The Peopling of Planet Earth

Human Population Growth
◊ Through the Ages ◊

ROY A. GALLANT

MACMILLAN PUBLISHING COMPANY
New York

COLLIER MACMILLAN PUBLISHERS
London

Macmillan Publishing Company
866 Third Avenue, New York, NY 10022
Collier Macmillan Canada, Inc.
First Edition
Printed in the United States of America
10   9   8   7   6   5   4   3   2   1
The text of this book is set in 11 point Sabon.
Maps by Andrew Mudryk

Library of Congress Cataloging-in-Publication Data
Gallant, Roy A.
The peopling of planet earth: human population growth
through the ages / Roy A. Gallant.—1st ed.
p.   cm. Bibliography: p. Includes index.
Summary: Examines the impact of human population growth,
discussing the origins of the human species, the rise of cities,
migration to the new world, population trends, and the
scarcity of natural resources.
ISBN 0-02-735772-4
1. Population—Juvenile literature.
2. Population—History-Juvenile literature.
[1. Population. 2. Population—History.] I. Title
HB883.G35   1990   304.6—dc20   89–34575 CIP AC

ACKNOWLEDGMENTS

I wish to thank Dr. Robson Bonnichsen, Director of the Center for the Study of the First Americans, University of Maine at Orono, for reading the manuscript of this book for accuracy. My thanks also to Dr. Frank Whitmore, paleobiologist with the Smithsonian Institution's Museum of Natural History, Washington, D.C., for reviewing selected sections of the manuscript, and to Dr. Edward J. Kormondy, ecologist and Chancellor of the University of Hawaii at Hilo, also for reading selected sections of the manuscript.

Macmillan Publishing Company has kindly given me permission to adapt excerpts from three of my earlier books, *Before the Sun Dies: The Story of Evolution; Earth's Changing Climate;* and *How Life Began: Creation versus Evolution,* the latter two published originally by Four Winds Press of Macmillan and all three of which are copyright by Roy A. Gallant. The Quotations from Thorkild Jacobsen are from his account of the *Enuma Elish,* in *The Intellectual Adventure of Ancient Man,* by H. and H. A. Frankfort, John A. Wilson, Thorkild Jacobsen, and William A. Irwin, Copyright © The University of Chicago Press, 1946. Those passages from the *Enuma Elish* itself are from A. Heidel's translation of *The Babylonian Genesis,* The University of Chicago Press, 1951. The account of the Pomo Indian creation myth is based on J. de Angulu's account in the *Journal of American Folklore,* Vol. 48, 1935. And finally, I am indebted to scores of researchers in the fields of anthropology, archaeology, evolutionary biology, paleontology, population ecology, demography, climatology, and other disciplines. The names of some of those researchers and writers, along with some of their published titles, are found at the end of this book in the section "Further Reading."

For Jon and Rosemary

Man is now, whether he likes it or not, and indeed whether he knows it or not . . . the sole agent for the evolutionary process on earth. He is responsible for the future of this planet.
—*Sir Julian Huxley*

Where Did the World's People Come From?

How many people were there "in the beginning," some 100,000 years ago when our human species, *Homo sapiens sapiens,* evolved? Two, a hundred, a hundred thousand, a million? What did they look like? How and where did they live, and how did they eventually come to populate virtually all corners of the planet: from the African plains to 15,000-foot heights in the Peruvian Andes, from the icy Arctic to humid tropical forests in Southeast Asia and the hot dry deserts of the Middle East?

Ten thousand years ago the total world population probably was no more than about 5 million people, the present population of the state of Missouri. Today the total world population is more than 5 billion and climbing faster than ever. How many more people can the planet feed and otherwise support in comfort? Some say that the planet can support 30 billion people. Others say that the population has already exceeded the optimal number, the number who can enjoy a "comfortable" life. But who is to determine what a "comfortable" life is for the world population? An African Bushman's idea of comfort is quite different from that of a Texas oil billionaire.

Many times in history, as local population explosions have occurred in large cities, disease has spread rapidly out of control and killed off large numbers of people, reducing a city's, a province's, or a nation's population to a mere skeleton of its former self. At various times during the fourteenth century the bubonic plague, or Black Death, killed between 25 and 50 percent of the population of Europe. In the year 1331 a plague epidemic in China's province of Hopei reportedly killed nine-tenths of the population. Between 1596 and 1602 half a million people are said to have died of plague in Spain. Are widespread disease and death nature's way of controlling runaway population growth? If so, what will be the long-term results of our medical technology's keeping more and more people alive and increasing life spans, thus adding to the human population cargo of spaceship Earth? Is medical technology a blessing or a curse to society?

These are not easy questions to answer, and experts often disagree about the impact of the world's human population explosion on the planet's future. Many more such concerns will be raised in this book. We will start with a haunting question that all people of every culture have pondered for thousands of years and that must be the starting point in our story of the peopling of planet Earth: How did human life begin?

Contents

The Peopling
of
Planet Earth

CHAPTER ONE

Human Origins: Supernatural Accounts

Myths are fossil religion. They are not the work of imagination, but the result of inter-preted observation. In them a great store of ancient and direct experience is laid up. And behind this fossil faith there is fossil history; actual happenings which lie far beyond the scope of history proper.

—*H. S. Bellamy*

THE ROLE OF MYTH

Is there a thinking person who has never asked, "How did life begin?" The question touches us deeply because, lurking within it, lies the very idea of our own human origin.

Questions of the origin of life and the peopling of the world are not the product of twentieth-century science, but are as old as human intelligence and have had nearly as many answers as there have been cultural groups spread over the world for the past 100,000 years and more. The fact that those answers had their roots in a belief in the supernatural is not important. What is important is that the questions *had* to be asked, and answers *had* to be found. The inquisitive nature of human beings made it so.

No culture that we know of is without its myths. The myth makers of former ages, troubled by unfamiliar and unexplained events in this

1

mysterious universe, eased their minds by interpreting the world through their myths. Because myths veiled certain disturbing aspects of reality, they saved man from racking his brains to solve problems that had no real solutions, at least at the time. They provided a kind of counterfeit experience that masqueraded as reality.

CREATION OF THE WORLD

One of the oldest accounts of the creation of the world takes us back five thousand years and more to the land of the Babylonians between the eastern end of the Mediterranean Sea and the Persian Gulf. This is the land of the biblical Garden of Eden and the hanging gardens of Babylon, the home of Abraham, traditional founder of the Hebrew people, and the setting for the *Arabian Nights* fables.

The creation myth of the Babylonians goes by the formal name of *Enuma Elish,* which means simply "when above," but it is popularly known as the "Babylonian Genesis." As old as the *Enuma Elish* is in its Babylonian form, it bridges back to a still earlier time, to a people known as the Sumerians, who were conquered by the Babylonians in 2000 B.C. The Babylonians, it seems, took over the plot of the *Enuma Elish* from the Sumerians and then cast their own, newer gods in the old Sumerian roles.

THE CHIEF SUMERIAN GODS

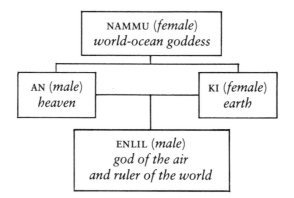

THE CHIEF BABYLONIAN GODS

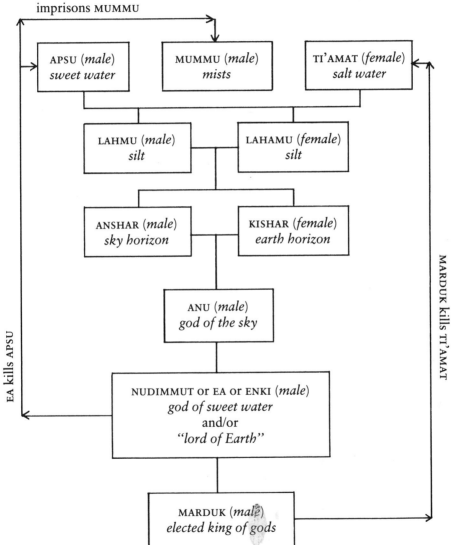

ACCORDING TO THE ENUMA ELISH

In the beginning, according to the *Enuma Elish*, there was only a chaos of water: "sweet" (meaning fresh) water of the land represented by the great god Apsu; salt water of the sea represented by the goddess Ti'amat; and cloudy mists represented by a third spirit, Mummu. The three kinds of water were at first mingled in a single mass, and there was no sky above or earth below, only the watery chaos.

The first lines of the *Enuma Elish* quickly establish the key gods who gave form to the world:

> When a sky above had not [yet even] been mentioned
> [And] the name of firm ground below had not [yet even] been
>   thought of;
> [When] only primeval Apsu, their begetter,
> And Mummu and Ti'amat—she who gave birth to them all—
> Were mingling their waters in one;
> When no bog had formed [and] no island could be found;
> When no god whosoever had appeared,
> Had been named by name, had been determined as to [his]
>   lot,
> Then were gods formed within them [that is, within Apsu,
>   Mummu, and Ti'amat].

Eventually, however, the two gods Lahmu and Lahamu were produced from the marriage of Apsu and Ti'amat. Scholars of the *Enuma Elish* think that Lahmu and Lahamu represented silt, or sediments, carried by the waters of the Tigris and Euphrates rivers. These two gods gave birth to Anshar and Kishar, who represent "the horizon," one a circle enclosing the sky and the other a circle enclosing Earth. Anshar and Kishar gave birth to the sky god Anu, who of himself gave birth to Nudimmut (or Enki), god of the sweet waters. However, Enki, also called Ea, had another aspect, that of a god who ruled Earth. Both sky and Earth were regarded as disks, with the Earth disk floating in the world-ocean. That view of the world persisted until the time of the early Greeks.

So in the Sumerian-Babylonian creation timetable, the first "geological" event to take place was formation of the first world-stuff, or silt. It came from the mingling of the fresh waters and the salt waters and took shape as a huge circle, the horizon, which year by year grew as more and more silt came into being and gave rise first to the sky and then to Earth. Pictured as two huge disks stuck together, the sky and Earth eventually were separated by the wind, and the region between them somehow inflated into an enormous closed volume of space. The upper surface became the sky and the lower surface the ground. All was surrounded by the primeval waters of chaos out of which all things living and nonliving originated.

The *Enuma Elish* myth goes on at great length, describing restlessness and then conflict among the gods, leading eventually to a feeling among them that a new king god must be found. The trouble begins when the lesser gods gather and dance wildly, whereupon the three chief gods, Apsu, Mummu, and Ti'amat, resolve to put down this new boisterous behavior. Apsu says:

> Abhorrent have become their ways to me,
> I am allowed no rest by day, by night no sleep.
> I will abolish, yea, I will destroy their ways,
> that peace may reign [again] and we may sleep.

The lesser gods are enraged when they learn of Apsu's plan. Ea kills Apsu and then imprisons Mummu, which leaves the powerful Ti'amat still free. How is Ti'amat to be subdued? Neither Ea nor any of the other gods is up to the task of defeating her, it seems. A new king god must be found, a god powerful in authority and at the same time physically strong enough to defeat Ti'amat in battle. In the Sumerian version of the myth, the young god elected by the council of gods is the robust god Enlil, but in the later Babylonian version Ea's son, the Babylonian god Marduk, is made the hero. So Marduk is to be armed and sent into battle against Ti'amat, who represents the universal and all-powerful sea.

Meanwhile, Ti'amat's forces meet in council and draw up their plans to do battle with the young, upstart gods:

> Angry, scheming, restless day and night,
> they are bent on fighting, rage and prowl like lions.
> Gathered in council, they plan the attack,
> [Ti'amat]—creator of all forms—
> adds irresistible weapons, has borne monster serpents,
> sharp toothed, with fang unsparing;
> has filled their bodies with poison for blood.
> Fierce dragons she has draped with terror,
> crowned with flame and made like gods,
> so that whoever looks upon them shall perish with fear.

To make a long myth short, Marduk first defeats Ti'amat's army and then confronts Ti'amat herself, who has assumed the form of a monster. After enclosing Ti'amat in his net, Marduk commands the wind to hold her powerful jaws open just when she is about to swallow him. He fires an arrow through her mouth and into her heart. Next he mashes her skull, thoroughly bleeds her, and finally cuts her body into two pieces. Marduk raises up one half of Ti'amat's body and with it forms the sky anew. There he establishes his home after making certain that the sea water still filling her hacked-up body will not come cascading out.

According to the scholar of Sumerian antiquities Thorkild Jacobsen, we can see in the *Enuma Elish* a basic attempt to account for certain events commonly observed by anyone living near the Persian Gulf in ancient Babylonia:

> The speculations which here meet us, speculations by which
> the ancient Mesopotamians thought to penetrate the mystery
> concealing the origin of the universe, are obviously based
> upon observation of the way in which new land is actually
> formed in Mesopotamia. Mesopotamia is an alluvial country.
> It has been built through thousands of years by silt which has
> been brought down by the two great rivers, the Euphrates

and the Tigris, and has been deposited at their mouths. This process still goes on; and day by day, year by year, the country slowly grows, extending farther out into the Persian Gulf. It is this scene—where the sweet waters of the rivers meet and blend with the salt waters of the sea, while cloud banks hang low over the waters—which has been projected back into the beginning of time. Here still is the primeval watery chaos in which Apsu, the sweet waters, mingles with Ti'amat, the salt waters of the sea; and here the silt—represented by the first of the gods, Lahmu and Lahamu—separates from the water, becomes noticeable, and is deposited.

Jacobsen reminds us that the Babylonians and the Sumerians before them turned to myth when they were unable to explain the annual flooding of the Tigris and Euphrates rivers that occurred regularly in their land. With the coming of each seasonal flood, they saw their small world threatened. Possibly it was about to revert to the "primeval watery chaos," but it never did. Each year the winds blew and drove the water away, just as they had dried up Ti'amat's blood after she had been hacked to pieces by Marduk.

CREATION OF LIFE

The *Enuma Elish* describes Marduk's many other tasks of creation after he has slain Ti'amat. He sets the stage for a calendar by creating the constellations and regulating their periods of apparent rising and setting, as he did for the Sun and Moon. Then he decides to free the gods of all menial tasks and to transfer those tasks to newcomers in the world, human beings, whom Marduk then creates.

He begins by assembling all the gods and asking them who incited Ti'amat to wage battle against them. When told that it was Kingu, Ti'amat's second husband, the assembly orders Kingu to be bound and executed. Then under the direction of Marduk's father, Ea, ruler of Earth, man is created:

I will create Lullu, "man" be his name,
I will form Lullu, man.
Let him be burdened with the toil of the gods, that they may
     freely breathe. . . .
They bound [Kingu], held him before Ea,
Condemned him, severed his arteries.
And from his blood they formed mankind.
Ea then toil imposed on man and set gods free.

The liberation of the gods takes place, and the gods are assigned to Anu, god of the sky. As a tribute to Marduk, the gods' final labor is to build him a magnificent temple in the sacred city of Nippur. The temple is to be a combination banquet and assembly hall where the gods can gather when they are summoned to discuss and rule over Earthly affairs.

In the conclusion of the *Enuma Elish,* Marduk's place as king of the gods and ruler of the world is assured for eternity, and people are instructed to honor their gods. As long as this is done, the world will continue as an orderly place and people will remember the great conquest of order over chaos.

CREATION MYTHS OF OTHER CULTURES

Common to virtually all creation myths are pairs of opposites: heaven and earth, good and evil, chaos and order, male and female, life and death, day and night, and so on.

According to a Chinese creation myth, in the beginning there was nothing. Then nothing turned into something, and that something became two parts, one male and the other female. This maleness and femaleness gave rise to another pair of unidentified substances, which in turn produced the creator-god P'an Ku, a grotesque being with horns (the Chinese symbol of supernatural beings), fangs, and a body covered with long hair.

P'an Ku's first task as creator was to bring order out of chaos by chiseling the primeval universal substance apart and separating it into sky and land. Next, he sculpted Earth's surface so that it had mountains, valleys, and rivers. He also created the stars. But to complete the scene P'an Ku had to die. His skull provided the perfect dome for the sky; his flesh became Earth's rich soil; his bones turned into the rocks; and his blood formed the rivers and seas. Trees and all other vegetation grew from his hair. The wind was his breath, thunder his voice, the Moon his right eye and the Sun his left, and his saliva turned into rain. Humans were created out of the vermin that covered P'an Ku's body.

The similarity among certain creation myths, but not necessarily among others, suggests that people have long been wanderers, distributing their wares and cultural baggage far and wide. For example, compare this Scandinavian myth with the P'an Ku myth:

Ymir was the first living being, a giant fashioned out of frost. The chief god Odin and his two brothers killed Ymir and made Earth out of his flesh, its oceans out of his blood, the mountains out of his bones, and the trees, grasses, and all other plants out of his hair. Ymir's huge skull formed the sky dome above, and sparks within his head were scattered as the Sun, Moon, and stars. To this day, Ymir's brain broods over Earth as fog and dark rain clouds that hang low, characteristic of certain coastal regions of Scandinavia. At Odin's command, dwarfs that live eternally underground and make beautiful jewels were created out of the maggots in Ymir's dead flesh. Meanwhile, the gods made the first man, named Ask, out of an ash tree, gave him life, a soul, his five senses, blood, and a power of motion. They likewise fashioned the first woman out of an elm tree and named her Embla.

In a number of creation myths the creator fashions humans out of bits and pieces of his own dead skin. For example, a Bagobo folktale from the Philippines refers to a white god with gold teeth who continually rubbed his skin to keep it white and in the process accumulated a mound of rubbed-off dead skin. Eventually, when the heap was large enough, he made Earth out of it; with the leftover bits he fashioned people.

The Pomo Indians of California tell of Madumda, identified simply as an "old man," who scraped dead skin from his body and formed it into a little ball before he went to sleep. Then after eight days he awoke, by which time the little ball had grown and become Earth, whereupon Madumda hurled it off into space. Because the world was so dark, Madumda next created the Sun by blowing a spark from his pipe into the sky. Next he walked around Earth and provided it with its features:

> "Here a mountain, here some rocks," he said. "Now a valley, a lake, clover growing, acorns on the mountains, juniper and cherries. There must be potatoes and rabbit," he said, "and on that mountain over there, let there be bear, puma, wolf, coyote, fox, skunk; on this one rattlesnakes, king snakes, garter snakes."

On noticing that one side of a mountain was always in shadow, Madumda was disturbed and felt that sometimes it should be lighted. After thinking about the matter for a while, he commanded Earth, "Roll over!" As it turned, that part of the mountain that had been in shadow gradually became bathed in light. (It would be interesting to know just how old this creation myth is, since it implies that its inventors presumed, and correctly so, that Earth's rotation on its axis, not a moving Sun, is the cause of day and night.)

When he had finished forming Earth's rivers, springs, and mountains and had caused trees, bushes, and other plants to grow, Madumda created the people. First he created feathers and then scattered them into the air, whereupon they became bird-people. Out of hairs plucked from his body he created the deer-people, the bear-people, and other four-legged animals. Then out of pieces of dried tendons that he took from a sack and broke into little pieces and scattered over the ground, he created humans. He then called all his people together and said, "This is your land. This is where you will live. There is plenty of food. Eat it." And he left.

In a second part, the myth describes Madumda's unhappiness when he returns and finds that the people are fighting each other and otherwise not behaving properly, and how he decides to destroy them by causing a universal flood. He then creates humans a second time, but as time passes these people, too, misbehave and so Madumda destroys them with fire. He destroys a third group of humans by causing an ice age to descend on them. Finally, he creates a fourth group and causes them to speak many different languages, and situates them all over Earth's surface. In this way he thinks he can keep them apart and so prevent their fighting one another. This time the bird-people, the fish-people, and all the others do as they are bidden, and Madumda leaves the world for the last time.

This myth has very close parallels to the Bible stories of the flood and the Tower of Babel. In the Bible, after the great flood has receded, Noah's descendants reach Babylonia and plan to build a tower reaching up to heaven. Disapproving of the idea, Jehovah foils the plan by causing the builders suddenly to begin speaking different languages so that they are unable to understand each other. And as the people speaking different languages separated and dispersed over Earth, eventually there evolved diverse cultural groups.

Like the Enuma Elish, numerous other myths relate the formation of the world out of a world-ocean. The oldest of the Egyptian creation stories, going back some six thousand years, says that in the beginning there was nothing but the primeval ocean, Nun, out of which the first god, the Sun god, created himself. Here, in contrast with some of the myths mentioned earlier, the first being was not produced through the union of a male and a female substance, but out of a sexless world-ocean. Before the Sun god came to rule over all of creation, he was called Atum, which means "everything" and "nothing." But on ruling he became known as Ra-Atum, *Ra* meaning "Sun." On rising out of the waters of chaos Atum said,

> Out of the abyss I came to be
> But there was no place to stand.

So he created a small mound of earth to support himself, and it became the world.

Next he created Shu, god of the air, and Tefnut, goddess of mois-

THE CHIEF EGYPTIAN GODS

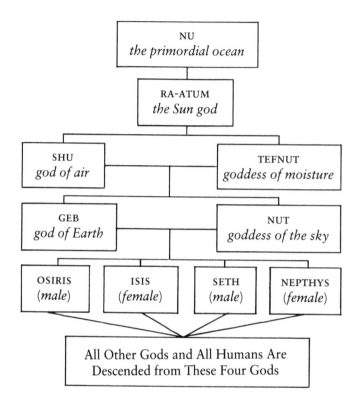

ture. From the union of Shu and Tefnut were born Geb, god of Earth, and Nut, goddess of the sky. Geb and Nut in turn produced the two gods Osiris and Seth and the two goddesses Isis and Nepthyus, from whom all the other Egyptian gods, and all humans, were descended. Because the Egyptians supposed that gods and humans alike were given life from the same source, they did not make a sharp distinction between them.

In other versions of the myth, Ra-Amon, a combination wind-Sun god, is cast in the role of creator, as are Ptah and Khnum in still other versions. Although the creator-god represents a different life force in each version, the story each myth tells is essentially the same: The Sun

The great Nile Delta, the dark fan-shaped area, is composed of silt yearly
carried seaward by the Nile River. The silt is a rich soil that has supported
farming along the Nile for many thousands of years. The Suez canal and
the Red Sea are seen above the Nile Delta.

plays the central role of creator. This idea turns up time and again in myths from all parts of the world that were invented by peoples who may never have had contact with each other.

Like the Sumerian myth makers, the Egyptians based their tale on what they could observe to be happening. Each year as the snows melted off the mountains in Ethiopia, the Egyptian segment of the Nile overflowed its banks and flooded the surrounding land from about July to October. After the flood waters had lowered, the silt carried by the river was left heaped up in little mounds: a re-creation of the small primeval mound of earth that Atum had created on rising out of the world-ocean. Within these small hillocks of slimy mud, a variety of living organisms would be found alive and well, warmed by the spring Sun. Here, then, was the original source of the world, quite likely "discovered" independently at different times and in different places by two ancient civilizations.

To early people, such mounds of earth appeared as if by magic; the people had no notion that the life-bearing sediment which so interested them had originated miles up river, far from where it was deposited in the river delta. And they had no way of knowing that life did not begin spontaneously in those small earth mounds once they were warmed by the Sun. At that time people didn't realize that the life in those mounds of sediments came from living things already there in the form of minute eggs and seeds. In the absence of such knowledge, it was natural to suppose that each year the Sun-creator reenacted its original role. Such myths, it would seem, are a blend of what actually was observed to take place and what people thought *should* have taken place. To put it in the framework of science, myth makers often draw incorrect conclusions from what they observe to be happening.

Human Origins:
Scientific Accounts

It is often said that all the conditions for the first production of a living organism are now present, which could ever have been present. But if (and oh what a big if) we could conceive in some warm little pond, with all sorts of ammonia and phosphoric acid salts, light, heat, electricity, etc., present, that a protein compound was chemically formed ready to undergo still more complex changes, at the present day such matter would be instantly devoured, or absorbed, which would not have been the case before living creatures were formed.

—Charles Darwin

SPONTANEOUS GENERATION

Creation myths can neither be proved nor disproved, because they are beyond the realm of reality; therefore, they are beyond the testing of science. Science deals with the natural world, with things that can be weighed and measured; it cannot deal with gods, ghosts, and other aspects of the supernatural, which are without substance and cannot be measured. An example will make this clear.

In the mid-1600s it was popularly believed that life commonly arose fully formed out of nonliving matter, that flies and certain other creatures were born out of dust and mud or out of decaying meat and the flesh of dead fish. This idea was called "spontaneous generation" and is an illustration of drawing incorrect conclusions from something that seems to be happening.

To challenge and test the idea of spontaneous generation, the Italian Francesco Redi did experiments showing that maggots, for example, which are the larval stage of flies, are not generated spontaneously by rotting meat. The idea for his experiments came from something he had observed.

Redi had put three dead snakes in a box and from time to time examined them as they decayed. Soon he noticed that maggots were crawling over the decaying meat and eating it. After a while nothing was left of the snakes except their bones. Nineteen days after he had put the dead snakes in the box, many of the maggots became inactive and formed themselves into hard balls, what we now know to be the pupal stage in the life cycle of a fly. At the time, however, the idea of life cycles of insects was poorly understood. The idea of an animal's changing its form seemed difficult to accept.

Redi next put some of the maggot pupae into a jar to find out what would happen. About a week later each pupa broke open and out came an adult fly. Could it be, Redi asked, that the maggots are not created out of dead meat but hatch from tiny eggs laid on the meat by adult flies? It was a hypothesis, an educated guess, and he lost no time testing it.

He put a dead snake in one jar, a dead eel in another, dead flesh from a calf in a third, and some fish flesh in a fourth. Then he did exactly the same with four other identical jars. While he left the first set of jars open to the air, he tightly capped the second set. As he examined both sets each day, he noticed that flies were entering and leaving the open jars, and within a few days he also noticed that maggots were crawling over the meat in all four of the open jars. There wasn't a single maggot on any of the meat in the four closed jars.

Redi and others performed more experiments that seemed to seal the fate of spontaneous generation. It seemed certain that living things could be produced only by other living things. Biogenesis, the idea that life arises only from living things and not from nonliving matter, became one of the foundation stones of biology.

But old ideas die hard, and spontaneous generation was not yet finished. One of the culprits was the newly invented microscope, which revealed a whole new world of tiny organisms that could not be seen by the unaided eye. A major question was, How do *these* tiny creatures originate? Where did the hundreds of different kinds come from? Were they subject to the law of biogenesis, or, since they were so simple, could they be generated from nonliving matter? The whole argument of spontaneous generation opened up again, since it was impossible to observe any eggs or seeds from which these elusive microscopic organisms developed. If a few strands of hay were placed in pure water, a few days later the water would be swarming with the creatures.

Around 1700 Louis Jablot designed an experiment similar to those of Redi. He put some hay into a container of water and then boiled it to kill all living matter that it might contain. Then he poured half the boiled material into a second container and tightly sealed it. After a few days he examined the contents of both containers. While he couldn't find a single living thing in the material from the sealed container, the material from the container that had been left open swarmed with life. He concluded that any material that has been purified (boiled) cannot possibly generate life. The living organisms in the container that had been left open, he said, had drifted in from the air.

Still, stubborn believers in spontaneous generation argued that, of course, if you kept air away from a purified substance, life could not be generated. The reason, they explained, was that air contains a "special life-giving substance" that could not reach the material in the sealed jar.

Around 1800 the French Academy offered a prize to anyone who could settle the spontaneous generation argument. The famous French scientist Louis Pasteur, who lived from 1822 to 1895, was the one to do it. He agreed that the air contained a special life-giving substance, but not a magical one, not a supernatural one. It contained microorganisms—germs, microbes, bugs, bacteria, or whatever you want to call them. Pasteur showed that two things were true: First, that microorganisms from the air entering milk, wine, water, or meat broth are killed by a long enough boiling time; second, that on exposure to the air all such substances become infected with bacteria.

In a wonderfully simple experiment, Pasteur made a glass flask with a long curved neck that narrowed to a small opening (about the size of a pinhole). Milk, beef broth, or any other purified (boiled) substance put in these narrow-neck flasks remained purified even though air could enter the flask through the small opening. What happened was that when bacteria in the air drifted in through the tiny opening, they got trapped in the curved neck and stuck there. He showed that this was so by tilting the flask until some of the liquid ran down and sloshed around where the bacteria were trapped and was then allowed to run back into the main part of the flask. The bacteria also washed back and soon multiplied into a thriving colony.

Except in the minds of the superstitious, the idea of spontaneous generation was dead.

THE EVOLUTION OF LIFE

Today biologists generally agree that life, in fact, did evolve from non-living matter, but not in the way supposed by the seventeenth-century believers in spontaneous generation. Evolution is an established fact and the unifying principle of all biology. It is the expression of the various patterns of biological change that produces new species of plants and animals and eventually causes the success or failure of species. As evolution has occurred throughout Earth's past, it continues today, and will continue for as long as there is life on this planet.

In the early 1950s, a graduate student named Stanley Miller, working at the University of Chicago, designed an experiment to find out just what kinds of molecules might have been present some 4 billion years ago, before life arose on Earth. His starting point was a picture of Earth's early atmosphere, most likely containing gases including hydrogen, methane, ammonia, and water vapor. He circulated a mixture of those gases through a closed system of glass tubing and then bombarded the gases with lightning discharges for a week. The water vapor condensed as "rain," and the other gases dissolved in the water. When Miller drew off some of the solution and examined it, he found that a number of complex molecules had been formed, molecules that are needed by all living things. Among them were amino acids, which are the building blocks of proteins.

Since then other researchers—and high-sc.___ ___...istry students—have repeated Miller's experiment and have produced many interesting molecules. In fact, they have produced all of the simple building blocks of the complex molecules of living cells, including the molecules of various cell parts and the energy-rich molecules that drive the many chemical reactions that keep a cell healthy.

The amino acids, proteinlike substances, and other complex molecules that were formed naturally in Earth's early atmosphere, on its warm rocks, and in its shallow seas were a far cry from living matter. But over a few hundred million years those molecules followed chemical pathways that produced complex packets of life-giving molecules. The most important ones were deoxyribonucleic acid (DNA), ribonucleic acid (RNA), and protein. DNA is a cell's master planner and directs cell activity. RNA takes instructions from DNA and oversees the manufacture of protein molecules. Protein molecules are used by all cells for growth and repair of worn or damaged parts.

Once established, those sacs of DNA, RNA, and protein became the first living cells—bacteria. Without enemies in the environment, those early bacterial cells began to reproduce at an astonishing rate, since they had a limitless supply of energy and food. We have fossil evidence that bacterial cells were alive around 3.5 billion years ago. Eventually those single-cell organisms gave rise to a more complex kind of living cell which, in turn, formed colonies of multicelled organisms. By the beginning of that geological time period called the Cambrian, some 580 million years ago, there was a profusion of complex life forms including plants, numerous soft-bodied animals such as sponges, and others with hard outer coats such as the trilobites. Evolution had taken off in a grand style. It went on to produce countless species, many of which in time moved onto the land.

About 200 million years later, the first amphibians appeared and soon established themselves on land. But they were not complete land dwellers, because they had to return to the water during part of their life cycle to lay their eggs. Present-day amphibians must do the same and include frogs and salamanders, for example. Rulers of the land for some 50 million years, the amphibians gave rise to a new group of animals, reptiles, which were complete land dwellers and dominated the landscape for some 150 million years. Among the reptiles of old were the dinosaurs. Modern reptiles include lizards and snakes, for instance.

Mammals, which evolved from reptiles, made their appearance about 195 million years ago but for a long time were overshadowed by the dinosaurs. The earliest mammals were small ratlike animals the size of a large cat. Today's mammals include all those backboned animals that nurse their offspring and most of which have body hair. They include humans, whales, camels, dogs, and many other species.

By about 65 million years ago, mammals had taken over and ruled the land. Not long before this, the primate branch of mammals had evolved. (Primates include lemurs, monkeys, apes, and humans.) Eventually the primate branch split off into three groups, one of which gave rise to the hominoid branch, which includes only humans and apes. To date, the oldest known hominoid was a fruit-eating apelike animal weighing about 10 pounds that lived in Egypt some 33 million years ago. Although today the area is desert swept by howling winds, it was once a tropical forest that was home for this oldest known of hominoids in the direct ancestry of humans.

In the 1960s, the late anthropologist Louis Leakey and his wife Mary discovered the upper jaw of a skull with teeth having characteristics of human teeth. The teeth formed a curved row and consisted of four types—incisors, canines, premolars, and molars. The skull, found in Kenya, was dated at 14 million years. This creature was apelike in some ways and humanlike in others; it was assigned to the genus *Ramapithecus*, first discovered in India by G. Edward Lewis in 1935. It belonged to a widespread group that lived in Africa, Asia, Greece, Turkey, and Hungary some 6 to 8 million years ago. Experts today regard *Ramapithecus* as an advanced ape, not a primitive human.

After millions of years, some 5 to 6 million years ago the warm and humid African climate underwent a marked change to a cool and dry climate. The once rich forests of tropical Africa dried up and were replaced by sprawling grasslands dotted by clumps of low trees. Unable to cope with the climate change, many species of forest animals and plants became extinct, but the new conditions favored an explosion of new species adapted to a grasslands habitat. Among them may have been a new line of primitive hominoids, called *Australopithecus*, meaning "southern ape."

Much younger than *Ramapithecus*, *Australopithecus* types keep turning up in Africa. The first was identified in South Africa by the anatomist Raymond Dart in 1924 and was between 1 and 2 million years old. It was the skull of a six-year-old child with distinctly human teeth. The oldest *Australopithecus* fossil remains found to date are about 3.5 million years old. They were uncovered in Hadar, Ethiopia, in 1974 by anthropologists Donald C. Johanson of the Cleveland Museum and Tim D. White of the University of California at Berkeley. The bones were of a female, named "Lucy" by the discoverers, who stood about 3 feet 8 inches tall and weighed about 65 pounds. In 1986, while digging in Olduvai Gorge, Tanzania (also in Africa), the same researchers found a skull and limb bones of a descendant of Lucy, about 1.8 million years old. The bones were those of a female of about 30, who stood about 3 feet tall. Members of her species are called *Homo habilis*, meaning "able man."

It is theorized that members of *Homo habilis* had learned to fashion crude tools out of pebbles, and that they supplemented their vegetable diet with meat. They lived in regions from Africa to Asia and in a short 200,000 years (1.6 million years ago) gave rise to the earliest known distinctly human line, called *Homo erectus*, meaning "upright man."

The interesting thing here is the rapid evolutionary change that took place in those 200,000 years. Evolution of the human line moved relatively quickly from a species only three feet tall (*Homo habilis*) to one nearly our size (*Homo erectus*).

The establishment of *Homo erectus* on the evolutionary landscape brings us to one of many times when glaciers crept overland and covered large areas of North America and Europe. In the process, dramatic changes in world climate patterns reshaped the lives and distribution of many species of animals and plants, as they had some 5 million years before in Africa. The glaciers also served as geographical "barriers" that discouraged or made impossible the exploration of distant lands.

The influence that climate and geological upheavals have had, and continue to have, on the evolution and distribution of plant and animal populations through time cannot be overemphasized. Geological events, such as the splitting apart of continents, are known to trigger major changes in climate, which in turn influence the spread and well-being of populations. The series of ice ages over the past few millions of years may have been caused by Antarctica's splitting off from the large southern continental land mass of Gondwana some 135 million years ago and drifting to its present position at the South Pole some 65 million years ago. The slow accumulation of the Antarctic ice cap gradually changed a generally warm and humid global climate favorable to the reptiles during the heyday of the dinosaurs to a cool and dry climate favorable to the rapid evolution of mammals when the dinosaurs became extinct.

The glaciation that gripped the Northern Hemisphere between 2 and 3 million years ago has continued off and on right up to the present. Several ice ages have come and gone over the past million years alone. Over the past 700,000 years, according to climatologist Reid A. Bryson, seven ice ages have alternated with interglacial warmer periods. It seems that we in the Northern Hemisphere may be near the peak of such a warm, interglacial period now. If another ice age grips regions of the Northern Hemisphere again in a few thousand years and covers them with ice two miles thick, major global climate changes will occur and some major reshuffling of the population distribution of humans as well as of other species will be in store.

Although *Homo erectus* was well on the way to becoming modern humans, these hominoids still had the telltale apelike features of powerful jaws, a large face, and a prominent brow bone. But apes they were not. They may have worn animal pelts for warmth against the cold and knew how to fashion weapons and stone tools more advanced than those of *Homo habilis*. Their brain size also increased, a fact that probably contributed to a use of language between 300,000 and 400,000 years ago.

Sometime before about a million years ago, members of *Homo erectus*—who were fully human, although they were not modern humans—began spreading from Africa into India, Southeast Asia, and China, because they wanted to and probably had to. They wanted to because their larger and more complex brains gave them a sense for exploration, a curiosity about what lay around that next bend in the river or over that distant mountain ridge. They most likely had to because of population pressure that forced many of them to seek a better living in new, uninhabited areas.

By at least a million years ago, these adventuresome humans had mastered fire, as shown by remains found in the Escale cave of southeastern France. It might have happened even earlier, for the researcher Robert Brian of the Transvaal Museum, Pretoria, South Africa, thinks he may have evidence of groups that mastered fire 1.7 million years ago. The control of fire revolutionized life. It enabled these early people to cook their food and carry heat wherever they went. It also provided a means of fending off predators at night, and gave light for the people to stay active for as long as desired beyond sunset. However, after being around for some 1.3 million years, *Homo erectus* became extinct 300,000 years ago.

In 1891, Eugene Dubois made the first fossil find of a *Homo erectus* descendant. It is known as Java man. In the 1920s a researcher named Davidson Black made another valuable find in China. There, a cave used by *Homo erectus* descendants for some 70,000 years revealed that these people were hunters. Among remains found in the cave were cooking hearths, tools, and many bones of the hunters themselves. Some of the bones included cracked-open skulls, suggesting that the hunters may have developed an appetite for human brains. It is just as likely, however, that the skulls were cracked open by earth pressure after they had been buried. This group of people is called Peking man. Similar fossil finds in Germany are known as Heidelberg man. All represent about the same stage in human physical and cultural evolution.

Is it possible that here we have the beginning, some 300,000 years ago, of the modern races of human beings, and that all evolved from the single widespread species *Homo erectus?* Eastern variants could have begun with Java man and Peking man, with western populations represented by variants resembling Heidelberg man.

Dr. Milford Wolpoff of the University of Michigan thinks that this probably is the case. "I'm one of many who conclude that modern humans originated in areas all over the world—after *Homo erectus* had populated that world and provided the basis for further evolution. And that, basically, modern Africans originated in Africa, modern Chinese in eastern Asia, modern Europeans in Europe. And this happened to some extent because all these populations were interconnected by a flow of genes. People were coming and going, exchanging wives, and so on. We think all humanity was interconnected this way," he says.

What conditions favored the evolution of language among groups of ape-men or man-apes or whatever we might call those early tool users and makers? As their activities became increasingly complex because of their mastery of tools and an expanding intelligence, perhaps the old primate system of animal calls, hoots, and grunts became too ambiguous and, therefore, became increasingly unreliable as a means of communication. Also, even a meager technology would require the identification of objects by name.

The new language that resulted did not replace the older and simpler language that may have consisted largely of emotional calls. Instead it added to the old language and rapidly developed in a new direction of language skills. It was through word language that humans were able to fashion culture and develop a self-awareness elevated above the level of physical comfort alone.

Out of that self-awareness, rooted in language, came the ability to develop value systems, and equally important, the ability to ask questions or make comments about the world, comments that were not only practical but intellectually stimulating for their own sake—a joke, a riddle, or a story. In short, language enabled humans to become creative in ways no other organisms could be.

CHAPTER THREE

Homo sapiens Takes Over

Is evolution a theory, a system, or a hypothesis? It is much more—it is a general postulate to which all theories, all hypotheses, all systems must henceforward bow and which they must satisfy in order to be thinkable and true. Evolution is a light which illuminates all facts, a trajectory which all lines of thought must follow.

—*Pierre Teilhard de Chardin*

MODERN HUMANS 100,000 YEARS OLD

The next major event in our story of the peopling of the world is the beginning of the take-over by modern humans. The time was some 300,000 years ago, during the last half of the Pleistocene epoch, which dates from about 2 million years ago. By that time the last *Homo erectus* types had disappeared and the human populations living in Africa and Asia were little different in appearance from populations living in those regions today. But if we met people of those Pleistocene populations we would notice some differences. They had larger jaws than ours, slightly longer heads, and somewhat larger faces. But because they were so much like us, we call them by our own scientific name *Homo sapiens*, which means "wise man."

The remains of four *Homo sapiens* types between 300,000 and 200,000 years old have been studied, two from France, one from Eng-

26

land, and one from Germany. Major differences in jaw size, ruggedness of body, and brain case size divided these populations. Had they remained isolated, separated by some geological barrier, eventually they might have evolved into separate species. But instead, there was mingling and interbreeding among certain of their populations. During that period a reduction of jaw size to that of modern people occurred among some of the groups.

The picture of how human beings evolved and populated various parts of the planet over the next 200,000 years is still hazy and much debated among anthropologists, although the paleontologist's spade continues to produce new evidence year by year.

By 115,000 years ago there seem to have been populations of people in southern Africa "totally modern in all observable respects, including the presence of a strongly developed chin," says University of Chicago anthropologist Richard Klein. The major South African site is Klasies River Mouth cave. Klein has worked at four additional South African sites that have yielded human fossils suggesting that modern human beings are at least 100,000 years old. Human fossil evidence found in a cave (Qafzeh) in Israel suggests that modern humans were living there around 92,000 years ago.

Among the relatively "less able" human types who seem to have been overcome by those early modern humans were many populations of large-jawed people who lived in Europe from about 100,000 to 35,000 years ago. Groups of them also lived in the Near East, and still other groups lived in southwest Asia until about 60,000 years ago. They are known as Neanderthals, and no hominids have been so abused and misunderstood as these people.

THE RISE AND FALL OF NEANDERTHAL

In 1856, fossils of Neanderthal man were unearthed in a limestone cave in the Neander Valley near Düsseldorf, Germany. These people lived in caves, as well as in the open in tents made of animal skins, and seem to have been the first to take up life in the wake of Europe's retreating glaciers. Many of the tools they left behind, including cutting tools and scrapers for cleaning animal hides, indicate that they were hunters and depended on the meat of ice age animals for food and on their skin for clothing and shelter. The tools were finer than those of *Homo erectus.* The Neanderthal brain case was a bit larger than ours, and their brain was probably just as well developed. They stood about five feet tall and had powerfully built bodies with large bones. "Their shin bones," according to writer John E. Pfeiffer, "could withstand bending and twisting forces which would snap our shinbones like dry twigs. . . . They had a hand grip two to three times stronger than ours, and their strongest individuals could probably lift weights of more than a ton."

Most likely descendants of *Homo erectus,* these people were enough like us to be given the scientific subspecies nametag of *Homo sapiens neanderthalensis,* and they spread across the Middle East and into western and central Asia. But Neanderthal became extinct about 35,000 years ago.

The mystery of this sudden disappearance, after Neanderthal had been around for some 65,000 years, has yet to be solved, but there are theories. Bone digs suggest that over a period of about five thousand years there was an overlapping of population territories between the large-jawed Neanderthals in Europe and their small-jawed neighbors who lived in the area of Israel and northern Iraq. These small-jawed types were nearly identical to us. Dress one of them in a jogging outfit and you wouldn't notice a difference.

One theory had it that the two populations interbred in the zone of overlap and so produced offspring of both the large-jaw and small-jaw types along with several other anatomical variations. But recent studies of Neanderthal anatomy suggest that there were enough differences between them and their small-chin neighbors to have prevented the Neanderthals from evolving into modern humans. Furthermore, the fact that the two populations lived side by side and preserved their distinct identities for so long makes it unlikely that the two types ever merged, biologically or culturally.

Could relatively rapid cultural and social advances among Nean-

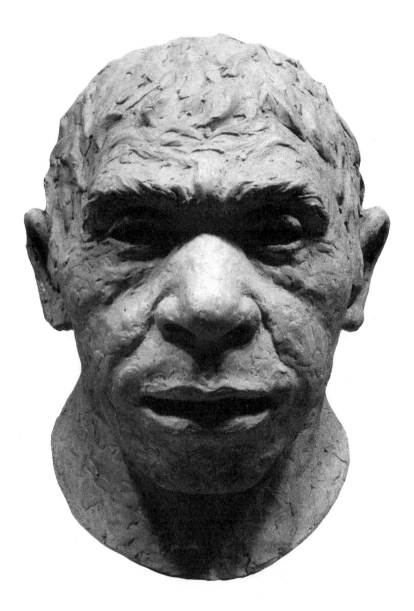

Neanderthal people had powerfully built bodies with large bones and stood about five feet tall. They roamed over Europe, the Middle East, and into western and central Asia over a period of some 65,000 years before they became extinct about 35,000 years ago. They buried their dead, controlled fire, made tools, and had brains capable of developing language.

derthal's modern neighbors have influenced Neanderthal's decline and eventual extinction? Some 30,000 and more years ago there was a burst of such cultural and social activity, as evidenced by prehistoric art discovered in caves in Brazil, Spain, and France. The cave paintings are of bison and other animals of the hunt, and their purpose seems to have been mystical, as if painting an image of the animal before a hunt would somehow bring the hunters good luck. Ritual and ceremony seem to have played an important role in the lives of the small-jawed populations of this time.

Humans have been picture-making animals for more than 30,000 years and have left their works of art in caves in Spain, France, Brazil, and many other places. This painting of a bison adorns a cave wall in Altamira, Spain.

This is not to say that Neanderthals were lacking in cultural practices. They were intelligent enough to have survived an Ice Age climate, and they seem to have been the first to bury their dead and believe in an afterlife. The fact that they did bury their dead is why we have so many Neanderthal remains. Several years ago archaeologists digging in the mountains of Uzbek in Central Asia uncovered a young boy's grave with 12 ibex horns marking his head. Is it possible that those Neanderthals of some 50,000 years ago had an ibex cult, as do the people living in the same region today?

For reasons unknown to us, about 50,000 years ago the Neanderthals began their journey down the one-way road to extinction.

CRO-MAGNON CAME TO STAY

Although there is no evidence for wars of extermination waged against the Neanderthals by their neighbors, by about 35,000 years ago all of the Neanderthals were gone. In their place, and populating Europe, Asia, and many other areas of the world, were groups of small-jawed people just like us, called Cro-Magnon, or *Homo sapiens sapiens.* Most of the world's human populations have diversified since *Homo sapiens sapiens* became permanently established, but some may still retain certain characteristics of the early *Homo sapiens sapiens* artists who left their cave paintings for future generations to interpret and admire. Among such groups are the Basque people of northeastern Spain, the Berbers of the Atlas Mountains in North Africa, and the African Bushmen.

During or after the extinction of Neanderthal, the newcomers fashioned many new tools of stone and bone: barbed harpoons, bone needles, spear-throwers, and numerous projectile points—stone spear tips, large and small, like those made by Paleo-Indians of the North American Southwest some 10,000 years ago. And they practiced the technique for mass killings of herds of animals—bison, for example—by causing them to stampede over cliff edges to their death. But this period of some 25,000 years after the extinction of Neanderthal is

The Paleo-Indians of North America conducted mass killings of bison by driving herds of the animals to their death over the edge of "buffalo jumps" like this one in Montana. For scale, note the size of the four cows grazing at the bottom of the jump. The author took this photograph from the edge of another buffalo jump.

frustratingly slim in evidence of *Homo sapiens sapiens*'s cultural progress. New evidence comes to light each year, however, especially in North and South America.

THE ORIGIN OF HUMAN RACES

Of the human species, the only one that survived the many snares of evolutionary, cultural, and technological competition is our own, *Homo sapiens sapiens*. There are no other human species, although there are various geographical races of modern humans.

A "race" within any species can be thought of as a group of populations that have certain genes and physical characteristics in common, which set that group of populations apart from all other populations of the same species. Genes are units of inheritance that we get from our parents and that determine what color eyes and hair we have, how tall we will be, and other traits. As *Homo sapiens sapiens* people increased their numbers and populated virtually every part of the world by about 50,000 years ago, their various populations gradually adapted to different regional environments and so evolved geographical races.

Populations of all organisms ebb and flow and change in response to changes in the environment, and they have done so throughout the history of life on this planet. Human populations are no exception, since our genes are subject to environmental pressures just as are the genes of other species. So human populations living in markedly different environments have adapted differently. For example, the Eskimos' relatively short fingers are thought to be an adaptation to a cold

Projectile points some seven inches long, such as this one flaked by striking on both sides, were notched in such a way that they could be fixed to the tips of spears. The Paleo-Indians of North America made the finest points of any culture some 10,000 years ago.

environment. Short fingers have less surface area from which to lose heat than do long fingers, so short fingers tend to lessen the risk of frostbite. On the other hand, people adapted to a hot climate tend to have long limbs, an adaptation that promotes heat loss and so prevents overheating of the body. Indians living in the Andes mountains of South America have evolved relatively large chests with larger lungs and a larger supply of blood than people living at sea level have. These features are adaptations to life at high altitude, where oxygen is harder to come by because of the lower atmospheric pressure.

The dark skin of the Negroid race may be an adaptation that protected the skin from the damaging action of ultraviolet radiation, which is more intense near the equator than in middle and high latitudes. So in that environment natural selection might have favored those individuals with the ability to produce lots of melanin, the pigment that darkens the skin. In medium and high latitudes where there is relatively less sunlight, a dark skin can be disadvantageous, however, since an excess of melanin interferes with vitamin D production in the skin through the action of sunlight. So natural selection at those latitudes, where there is relatively less sunlight than at the equator, might have favored individuals with the relatively light skin color of the Caucasoid race.

It is hard to pin down the origin and selective advantage (or disadvantage) of certain variations that have been used to establish the races. Furthermore, such variations are characteristic of *populations,* not of *individuals.* Because that is so, there always will be individuals who cannot be pigeonholed into the racial categories identified with the researchers Franz Weidenerich and Carleton Coon.

Those researchers supposed that the modern races of humans descended from old hominid lines that evolved independently into various racial groups: A Middle East type, perhaps Mount Carmel man, supposedly led to the Caucasoid (white-skinned) race; Rhodesian man to the Negroid (black-skinned) race; Peking man to the Mongoloid (high cheek bones and yellow skin color) race; and Java man to the Australoid (brown-skinned) race. Still another suggested racial category was the

Amerind (red-skinned). So at one stage in hominid history, according to the Weidenerich-Coon plan, there were a number of pure races, which over the centuries became increasingly blurred due to migration and intermixing.

You sometimes hear people speak of the Italian "race" or the Jewish "race." There is, of course, no such thing. There is a Jewish religion or a Catholic religion, people of Italian nationality or French nationality, but none of these is a *race*. You also sometimes hear of the Aryan "race," which is another mistaken idea. Aryans are people who speak languages that are offshoots of the root language Indo-European. Such languages include German, Italian, French, English, and others. So anyone who speaks one of those languages as a native is an Aryan. All such people belong to different cultures, not different races.

The idea that the modern human geographical races have evolved as a result of population adaptations over thousands of years is hard to challenge, even if some of the causes are not yet clear. When different populations of the same species go slightly but significantly separate ways in response to different environmental conditions, we call it parallel evolution. But those separate ways have never led to an unchanging human race.

There is no such thing as a "pure" race, meaning one that forever remains the same. Because all human beings belong to the same species, our various populations are capable of interbreeding, and interbreeding has been the rule throughout human history. Time and again, as invaders of one geographical race have conquered a neighboring people, the populations have mixed and their racial distinctions have blurred slightly. According to the evolutionary biologist E. Peter Volpe, "The distinguishing features of the basic racial groups have become increasingly blurred by the countless migrations and intermixings. The whole world today is a single large neighborhood. Modern man lives in one great reproductive community."

Races, then, are nothing more than temporary collections of genes in a population's "gene pool," temporary and passing stages in the evolutionary history of a species. To illustrate that point, consider what ecologists who study populations call "genetic drift," the reason some populations tend to remain pretty much the same, for a while at least, while others are characterized by rapid change.

GENETIC DRIFT

One way a population's gene pool can change is through genetic drift. Genetic drift is the loss of most of the genes in a small population's gene pool, with the result that the few remaining genes are those that form the basis of the gene pool as the small population rebuilds itself. This may occur when most individuals of a population are killed, which happens among alpine butterflies, for example, during a particularly harsh winter. The gene pool of these butterflies is seriously drained because there are fewer individuals to contribute their genes, so fewer genes and gene combinations are available as the population is rebuilt. This temporary loss of genetic variation tends to limit a population's ability to cope with harmful environmental change.

A special case of genetic drift involves a small religious sect called the Dunkers who live in eastern Pennsylvania. More than two hundred years ago a small group of Dunkers came to America from western Germany and ever since have clung to their customs, one of which prohibits marriage with outsiders. Nearly ten generations of maintaining their small gene pool have led to a number of interesting genetic traits. For instance, when compared with their relatives in Germany, and with the general United States population, the Dunkers have very few individuals with either B or AB blood types. The gene controlling those blood types has been nearly lost from their gene pool.

Another example of genetic drift involves a small population inhabiting the Pingelap atoll in the central Pacific Ocean. In the past the atoll has been devastated by typhoons and famine. In 1775 the island's population was reduced to a mere thirty individuals. Over the years that small population increased to about two thousand, but in virtual isolation and without the benefit of gene-pool enrichment by outsiders. As a result of their closed gene pool, about 5 percent of the population today inherits a form of color blindness that is extremely rare in the human population as a whole.

So geographical barriers, in the case of the Pingelaps, or cultural barriers, in the case of the Dunkers, tend to keep a population's gene pool pretty much the same. There are numerous other examples, including the Aborigines of Australia and the African Bushmen, who have kept their cultural barriers more or less intact over the centuries. The opposite condition can be seen in Hawaii today. A century or so ago the Hawaiians were a distinct culture, but since that time they have intermarried on a wide scale with Japanese, Chinese, and individuals of other cultures to the extent that only a handful of genetically true Hawaiians are left. Their gene pool is today widely varied, enriched by many new genes from other cultures.

From Hunter-Gatherers to Farmers

Overpopulation is the most serious threat to human happiness and progress in this very critical period of the history of the world. It is not so acute as the threat of atomic warfare, but is graver, since it springs from our own nature.

—Sir Julian Huxley

Today, the world over, most populations are growing at a rate that causes deep concern among many population ecologists. Runaway population growth is especially serious in areas including South America, Africa, and India, for example. At each beat of your heart a baby is born somewhere in the world. It doesn't take much arithmetic to figure out that that means 37 million new people—equal to the combined populations of the states of Washington, Oregon, California, Alaska, and Hawaii—are added to the planet every year. But human population growth, as you will find in the next chapters, has not always been as rapid as it is today. For most of our human history on Earth, population growth has been relatively slow.

FIVE MILLION HUNTER-GATHERERS

Ten thousand years ago was an important time in the history of human population growth. Before then there were no cities where thousands of people lived or gathered for religious or other ceremonies. At best, probably loosely associated groups of families, numbering a few hundred or less, interacted and set up temporary villages on a seasonal basis. Most continued to live as hunter-gatherers, people who wandered about killing what game they could find and eating vegetable matter, including seasonal berries, wild fruit, and nuts, as had their ancestors for more than 100,000 years. Others chose a somewhat more settled life in semi-permanent shelters of wood or animal skins, but they were still hunter-gatherers who prospered when game and food plants were plentiful and went hungry when food was scarce. A varied diet favored survival, whereas a diet that depended on only a narrow selection of foods must often have meant hardship.

When times were good, local populations tended to increase; when they were bad, populations just held their own, or declined. Whether times were good or bad, one out of every two infants died during the first year of life, of malnutrition, disease, or accidents. When there were still too many mouths to feed, infants were killed and abortions performed so that the group might survive.

Another solution to overpopulation was for some families of a group to strike out over the next ridge and into the next valley in search of new lands that might have abundant game. Imagine the disappointment of such groups if on reaching that faraway ridge they saw wisps of smoke from distant campfires down in the valley. Even 10,000 years ago the world may have seemed crowded with an estimated population of about 5 million. We can make that educated guess about population size on the basis of several clues; for example, by knowing the population densities of hunting and gathering tribes living in South America and Africa today, and by estimating that about 20 million square miles of Earth's surface were suitable for a hunting and gathering existence.

The world population grew only slowly over the next 9,000 years. The number of births has to be greater than the number of deaths if a population is to grow, and 10,000 years ago life was short and harsh. Most people could expect to die by the age of twenty or thirty. Before people learned the skills of farming, and so came to control their food supply, they were very much at the mercy of the environment. Until agriculture came to be practiced, the number of humans was probably limited in much the same way that the numbers of any other large predator are limited. The shift from food gathering to food growing and the domestication of animals some 10,000 or more years ago was a momentous change and meant that greatly increased numbers of people could be supported.

THE RISE OF AGRICULTURE

Skilled agriculture arose out of a need. Dwindling supplies of game as a result of extinctions at the end of the last ice age and increased hunting by an ever-growing world population must have made people more and more dependent on food plants as a source of nutrition. Over tens of thousands of years the hunter-gatherers had observed that wild plants grew from seed and had figured out that such growth could be controlled to suit the group's need when necessary—during times of game shortage or rapid population growth. Skills in agriculture that had arisen gradually over a very long time were simply waiting to be called on when needed.

That time came in several regions at different times. It came in northern latitudes some 14,000 years ago, when the end of the last ice age brought climate change in temperature and rainfall across North America, northern Europe, and elsewhere. That climate change also caused the extinction of many animal groups, including the mammoths, mastodons, giant sloths, North American horses, and saber-toothed cats. As glacial ice retreated northward, storm tracks changed, and desertification began in the Sahara, the Near East, and north central China. Climage change led to global restructuring of ecosystems, major extinctions like those just mentioned, and changes in human adaptive patterns. The hunter-gatherers had to adapt to the greatly changed environment or perish.

A researcher named Earl Saxon reported one example of how climate change affected the hunter-gatherer practice of a group of prehistoric people living along the coast between what is now Tel Aviv and Haifa. In one location Saxon found 1,300 animal bones, of which 1,000 were those of young gazelles two years old or younger. The bones were spread out in such a way to suggest that the hunter-gatherers were expert at managing herds of wild gazelles, much the way that Laplanders manage reindeer herds today. The gazelles were permitted to graze along the coastal plains and were killed selectively on a seasonal basis so that the herds were kept intact and healthy. Saxon thinks that such herd management had been going on for 30,000 years or longer. But with the melting of the ice sheets 14,000 years ago, sea level was raised so much that the coastal plains were flooded and the gazelle herds dispersed. To survive, the ancient Middle Eastern hunter-gatherers had to make their living another way, by depending on the rich stands of wild wheat and barley inland in the hills.

Some think that climate change at the end of the last glacial period reduced the population of Europe from about 500,000 to half that number. Over the next few thousand years many groups came to direct their energy and ancient knowledge of agriculture toward a more or less settled life of farming and so set in motion a cultural revolution that changed the world.

At first, farming groups probably had several seasonal "farms" that they visited in turn as various food plants ripened at different times throughout the year. Mexico's Tehuacan Valley and Peru's Ayacucho Valley are two such regions in the New World that must have made ideal seasonal farmlands.

Halfway around the world in Iraq, groups were growing wheat and barley and had domesticated goats, sheep, pigs, and cattle some 9,500 years ago. The idea and practice of maintaining herds of domesticated animals had many new and far-reaching benefits. Here is one interesting and important example. Children are born with the ability to digest milk because their bodies make lactase, the digestive juice, or enzyme, that processes milk sugar, lactose. But beginning 10,000 or so years ago, most people characteristically lost the ability to produce lactase on reaching adulthood and so lost the ability to digest milk, as is true for many to this day.

Then some Middle East populations "mysteriously" regained their ability to digest lactose in adulthood and so could use milk as a lifelong food. Their newfound ability probably was caused by a genetic mutation that produced the needed enzyme lactase in the intestinal tract. Once introduced into a population's gene pool, the lactase-producing gene spread to other individuals, and eventually was carried to other populations of the Middle East and farther afield. The ability to digest milk products provided a valuable new source of nutrition—animal protein without the need to kill the animal. It also provided a source of vitamin D. This mutation changed the course of history by encouraging the breeding of milk cows, the milking of goats and sheep, and the production of cheese, butter, and other milk products.

Agriculture was discovered independently and at different times in several parts of the world. Some 8,000 or more years ago Paleo-Indians living in the highlands of Mexico learned to cultivate maize (corn), which became the single most important food plant in the New World. By 5,000 years ago Indian farmers in central Mexico also were growing beans, squash, and other plants. About the same time, the Chinese along the Yellow River were growing millet and later grew rice. Farming villages also appeared in Egypt and elsewhere about this time. Controlled agriculture was to lead to permanent villages, intensive farming, the use of irrigation, and claims on certain areas that were fortified and defended against intruders.

Those groups that remained hunter-gatherers most likely did so because a hunter-gatherer existence required less labor than farming. Richard Lee, of the University of Toronto, reports that today the Kalahari Bushmen hunter-gatherers live on a nutritious diet of two-thirds nuts and vegetables and one-third meat, and they work only one to three days a week to feed themselves. During one of Africa's recent and most severe droughts, the Bushman hunter-gatherer tribes had plenty of food while their farmer neighbors faced starvation and had to rely on famine relief from the United Nations. Many survived only because they joined and adopted the ways of Bushman tribes.

The practice of growing food plants instead of simply gathering them spread rapidly after about 7000 B.C. Life was no longer only a matter of survival. Surplus food could be stored and used as needed, during times of drought, for instance. Food stores also meant that some members of a community could be released from farming chores and devote time and thought to other matters: the development of better weapons and tools, more ornate basketry and pottery, finer clothing and ornaments, better houses, more elaborate ceremonies, or intellectual skills such as writing, mathematics, and astronomy.

SOCIAL CHANGE BROUGHT BY FARMING

Settlement meant new kinds of social organization and bigger local populations to share in the large amount of labor needed in agriculture. It also meant that a reliable water supply was needed for crops, drinking, and sanitation. In various parts of the world elaborate irrigation systems were created, such as those great ditches dug by people of the Hohokam culture in central Arizona, the canal system of people living along the Peruvian coast, and the aqueducts made by the Incas of Cuzco, which still stand. Such massive engineering efforts required huge amounts of labor.

The human population began to soar wherever farming was practiced, because farmed land could produce fifty times more food than unfarmed land could, and because women living in settled communities could more easily have children and care for them.

Once local groups had outgrown the ability to support themselves by a hunter-gathering existence, they were committed to agriculture, like it or not. The wild land could no longer support the swelling numbers of people in the nutritional life-style they had come to know and expect. Going back to the ways of their ancestors would have meant certain starvation for most. What were once seasonal villages grew into permanent settlements, mushroomed in numbers and size, and soon gave rise to the first cities.

CHAPTER FIVE

The Rise of Cities: 1

Worlds on worlds are rolling ever
From creation to decay,
Like the bubbles on a river
Sparkling, bursting, borne away.
                    —*Percy Bysshe Shelley*

THE FERTILE CRESCENT

In this chapter we add a new thread to our story of human population growth: its short-term and long-term effects on the environment, beginning in the Near East, which saw the first widespread use of agriculture and the rise of the first cities and city-states.

We return to the land where, according to the *Enuma Elish*, the world began, a region that today is part of Iraq. Called the "Fertile Crescent," this land forms a seventy-mile-wide arc from the northeastern corner of the Mediterranean Sea down to the Persian Gulf. It is that once-fertile region between the two great rivers Tigris and Euphrates where Africa, Asia, and Europe meet. Some 2 million years ago, waves of prehumans spilled out of Africa and crossed this way into Southeast Asia and China, into the lands of the Mediterranean, and into northern Europe. It is also the region from which waves of knowledge spread like the rings of water sent outward by the toss of a pebble into a pond, and in only a few thousand years energized that cultural eruption we call civilization.

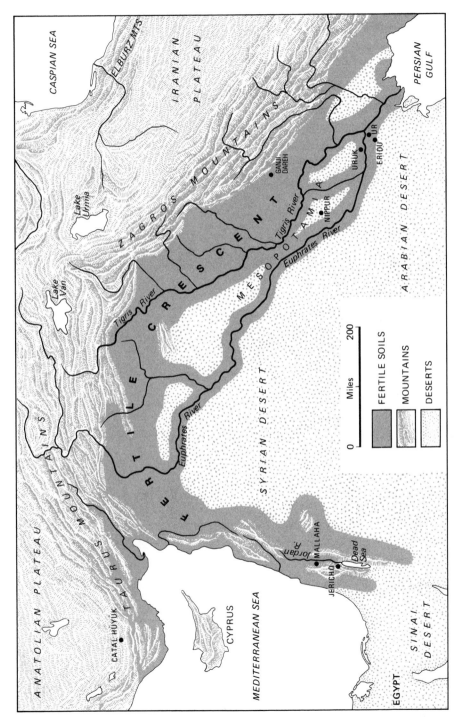

The "Fertile Crescent," an arched region south of the Black Sea that forms part of present-day Iraq, was once a rich garden area that supported abundant wildlife. Called the "cradle of civilization," today it is mostly desert, but a treasure house for the archaeologist's spade.

About 10,000 years ago hunter-gatherers in this region lived on plentiful supplies of wild grasses of wheat and barley and probably enriched their diet with the meat of wild goats, sheep, pigs, and cattle. Many of the two thousand known sites containing evidence of early agriculture have been found here. Twenty-five miles inland from the eastern shore of the Mediterranean is the 10,000-year-old site of Mallaha, excavated by the French archaeologist Jean Perrot. It contains many artifacts, including tool remains of small, sharp-edged cutting instruments and the remains of foundations for round houses and grain storage pits lined with plaster. The village contained possibly two hundred people and remained occupied for a thousand years.

Another site, Ganji Dareh, which lies three hundred miles northwest of the Persian Gulf and dates from 7300 B.C., shows unmistakable signs of domesticated animals, farming, and well-constructed buildings of straw-enforced bricks laid with precision.

Some 450 years earlier people had settled in Jericho near the Dead Sea. Jericho may have been one of the first trade centers in the world. Another trade center was the site Catal Hüyük in what is now southern Turkey. By 6000 B.C. Catal Hüyük was a busy center of some thirty acres with houses, ceremonial centers, and places of business where superb daggers of flint and figurines of limestone and clay were traded.

THE CITY OF URUK

As the rich region of the Fertile Crescent grew in population, encouraged by a highly productive agriculture aided by irrigation, more and more permanent settlements appeared. People began to cluster into ever-larger centers, which eventually became the first cities.

One such center was Uruk, the largest of some half-dozen cities established around 3500 B.C. in the ancient land of Sumer, home of Marduk and Ti'amat. The Uruk of 5,500 years ago was a vast garden of flowers, date palms, marshes teeming with wildlife, reeds, poplar trees, and artificial lakes and canals fed by the cool waters of the Euphrates River, which flowed past the city's gates. Over the millennia Uruk slowly crumbled to dust, but since the early 1900s the city has methodically been excavated and its secrets revealed by archaeologists from many nations.

In its prime, Uruk was surrounded by a twenty-foot-high wall six miles around. Made of sun-baked bricks, the wall had two massive gates and numerous watchtowers. Within were mud-brick houses, ceremonial centers, fields of cultivated wheat and barley, and grazing areas for sheep, goats, and cattle. Craftsmen mixed crushed reeds with river mud to make the bricks. One of Uruk's temples was made not of mud-brick but of limestone blocks cut and carried from a quarry thirty-five miles away.

Among the 20,000 people who lived in Uruk were peasant-farmers, craftsmen, builders, soldiers, priests to rule over ceremonial affairs, and the elite and privileged rulers with their many slaves and other luxuries. By this time in the city's history there were well-established social levels, or classes. Most of the back-breaking work, such as digging irrigation canals and moving stone blocks into place, probably was done by prisoner-slaves captured in battle. Female slaves most likely were given easier tasks such as spinning and weaving cloth, cleaning the temples, and attending to the wants and needs of their royal owners.

The many Sumerian gods—of the sky, earth, underworld, and so on—were worshipped in numerous temples, not only at Uruk, but at other temple-cities including Eridu and Ur. Remains uncovered at Ur provide grim evidence of human sacrifice carried out as a religious practice. For example, the famous Death Pit contains a king and queen buried with their most precious possessions and sixty-four richly dressed "ladies of the court." Funeral carts with the draft animals still harnessed to them, soldiers, servants, and girl musicians buried with their fingers on the strings of lyres, were all entombed with their dead ruler. In the Sumerian world humans existed to serve the gods.

SOCIAL ORGANIZATION

The rise of cities brought about several important social changes. Laborers had to be organized to work long hours not only for their own support, but also for the support of the high priests and other elite members of an emerging ruling class, which demanded the best of food, clothing, and other material comforts. These demands often were made in the name of service to the gods, hence the emphasis on establishing ever-grander temples of worship. As organized religion became more powerful, leaders found they could use spiritual influence for political ends and so keep the masses under control. In many instances—in the Near East and later in India, China, Egypt, and Mesoamerica, for example—in the eyes of the masses their rulers were sometimes raised to the level of divine beings to be worshipped. So there were two universal classes of rulers—mortal kings and divine kings.

By about 3500 B.C. many trade routes and trade centers had developed in the Near East, such as Malyan, which thrived between 3200 B.C. and 2800 B.C. Trade required that records be kept: how many of what kinds of objects and animals were sent overland by whom and to whom.

A system of numbers probably came before writing. According to archaeologist Denise Schmandt-Besserat of the University of Texas at Austin, the first counting systems might have been in existence some 10,000 years ago. At that time in the Middle East, people kept track of their cattle and other goods with little tokens of baked clay—two egg-shaped tokens for two jars of oil, four little spheres for four containers of grain, and so on. Only later, perhaps 5,000 years ago, did some budding mathematician make the quantum leap from counting specific objects such as jars of oil and cows to an abstract concept of numbers as an expression of pure quantity. And so the idea of recreational mathematics was born.

How to count in Babylonian

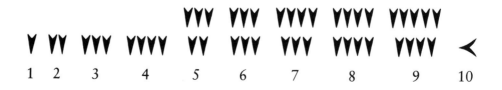

1   2   3   4   5   6   7   8   9   10

These early Indus Valley stamp seal imprints, showing a tiger, an elephant, and probably a god, bear a combination of pictures and writing. Earlier seals were simpler, imprinting plain designs such as triangles or circles.

Record keeping also required some form of writing. The earliest known "writing" took the form of simple pictorial seals that could be pressed into the soft clay of a pot or brick to identify its maker. Early seals were simple crosses, or human or animal forms, or geometric shapes such as triangles. More complex figures on seals came later as trade among villages increased. From the simple stamp seal evolved the cylinder seal, which could be pressed and rolled around the rim of a clay jar before it was baked and so provide not only a decorative design but one that unmistakably identified its owner. For instance, a trader who dealt in wool might use a seal that showed men driving a herd of sheep.

Such pictograms, which resulted partly from the record-keeping needs of trade, represent a beginning stage of writing. The earliest known true writing appears on clay tablets from Uruk dated around 3500 B.C. They contain inventory lists of goods and records of astronomical events with symbols of the planet-gods. By this time the inventors of cuneiform writing, as this early writing is called, were working with about two thousand different signs, including pictograms of animals, wheat, the Sun and Moon, and other objects. The invention of writing—which arose independently in many cultures—marked the end of prehistory and the beginning of recorded history.

The rise of cities was made possible by controlled agriculture and was kept in a state of economic order by the invention of writing. The

The first writing known to us is that of the Sumerians and is dated around 3500 B.C. Wedge-shaped marks pressed in soft clay tablets were used to record inventory lists of goods and to make records of astronomical observations, including the Sun, Moon, and planets.

In these examples of signs used in early forms of writing, some of the signs, such as those for "bull" and "barley," resemble the objects they represent while others do not.

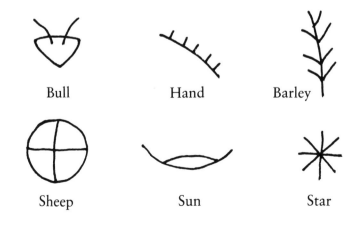

Bull   Hand   Barley

Sheep   Sun   Star

rise of cities marked the beginning of a race between population growth and the availability of an adequate food supply—a race against starvation, which once started could not be stopped and which continues to this day. Although many experts think that the early practice of agriculture triggered rapid population growth, others such as the economist Ester Boserup think that rapid population growth came first and prompted the widespread practice and development of agriculture. This argument has yet to be resolved by anthropologists.

By about 3000 B.C. the estimated world population was some 100 million, and the population of the Fertile Crescent may have been about 20 million. Of these at least a third were still hunter-gatherers who lived outside the urban centers and who sometimes traded with and sometimes raided the city dwellers. A typical nomad group of this time may have consisted of half a dozen families of thirty or forty people, and seventy or so sheep and goats.

EAST TO OTHER LANDS

Moving southeast across what is now Iran and Pakistan to the Indus River Valley brings us to the next region to practice organized agriculture and a way of planning cities that took a turn different from that of cities of the Near East.

By at least 300,000 years ago, people from Africa had made their way into India, where they left certain kinds of tools that had evolved from an earlier African technology. But the first evidence of residents of India having domesticated animals, including dogs, sheep, goats, cattle, and pigs, dates from about 5500 B.C. The 7,500-year-old site bearing evidence of such people is at Adamgarh, some four hundred miles northeast of Bombay.

Not until 4000 B.C. to 3500 B.C. do we find settled farmers in small villages tilling the fertile soil of the Indus Valley. By this time the Near East city of Uruk was thriving. But once they started, the Indus Valley residents bridged the gap between settling down in villages and building their first cities in only a thousand years. It had taken the

In the early 1920s Sir John Marshall uncovered many copper tablets from Mohenjo-Daro containing a mixed pictorial (top) and syllabic script.

people of Sumer twice that long. And compared to the cities of the Near East, those of the Indus Valley almost seemed to follow an architect's model.

In place of the twisting narrow streets of Uruk, the Indian cities of Mohenjo-Daro and Harappa had long straight streets the width of two superhighways with cross streets at right angles. Oriented north-south and east-west, the broad streets were lined with luxurious houses containing baths, lavatories, drainage and fresh-water tanks, elaborate inside courtyards, guest rooms, dining rooms, and servants' quarters. Quite "modern" at a time when central Europeans were still living in caves, these two cities prospered between 2500 B.C. and 1750 B.C. Both are the first known examples of city planning. The population of Mohenjo-daro, which covered some 240 acres, probably reached 30,000 at its peak.

Mohenjo-daro and Harappa, about 350 miles distant from each other, were two of four major cities that controlled the first Indus state. In addition to the cities, there were about twenty smaller outlying centers and two hundred villages that sprawled over an area of more than 400,000 square miles. At its peak around 2000 B.C., the Indus state may have contained a quarter of a million people. That would mean a population density of 1.6 people per square mile. In 1989 the combined population of India and Pakistan reached 945 million. That results in a population density of more than 500 people per square mile.

The Indus Valley population began to swell as increasing numbers

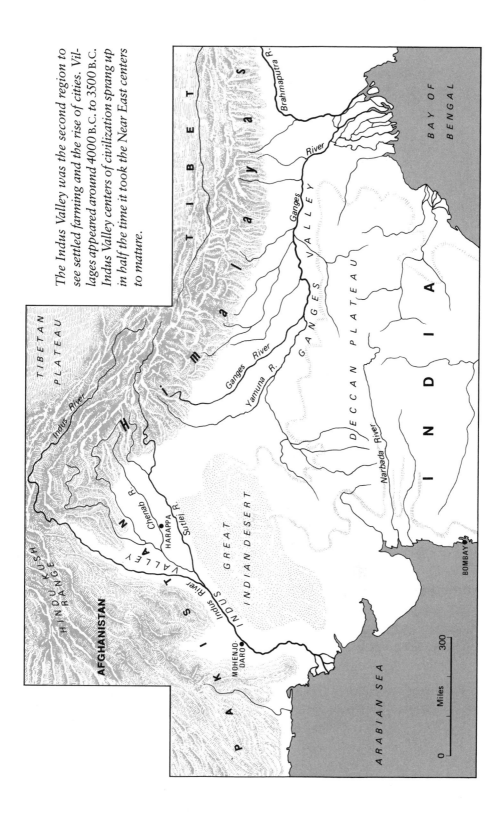

The Indus Valley was the second region to see settled farming and the rise of cities. Villages appeared around 4000 B.C. to 3500 B.C. Indus Valley centers of civilization sprang up in half the time it took the Near East centers to mature.

TIBET

TIBETAN PLATEAU

H i m a l a y a s

Brahmaputra R.

River

Ganges

GANGES VALLEY

Ganges River

Yamuna R.

Indus River

HINDU KUSH RANGE

AFGHANISTAN

INDUS VALLEY

Chenab R.

Sutlej R.

HARAPPA

GREAT INDIAN DESERT

MOHENJO-DARO

DECCAN PLATEAU

Narbada River

INDIA

PAKISTAN

BOMBAY

BAY OF BENGAL

ARABIAN SEA

Miles

0   300

of nomadic hunter-gatherers, also feeling the pressure of population growth, came down out of the mountains for a less competitive life on the fertile lowlands. India probably had begun to feel population growth pressure as early as about 3600 B.C., just before its first cities began to rise. The most rapid growth then seems to have come around 2000 B.C. when the Indus state reached its peak. A similar pattern had occurred in the Near East about five thousand years earlier, and it was to occur later in other parts of the world as population growth on the planet continued to gain momentum.

Before continuing our way eastward into southeast Asia, China, and across the Pacific to the New World to find out when and how those regions developed, we should introduce the notion of the "carrying capacity of the environment." We have already touched on this concept, and it will come into play more and more in the following chapters.

CARRYING CAPACITY OF THE ENVIRONMENT

The ups and downs of any population—animal and plant species alike—depend on how the population reacts with its environment. In 1798 the English economist Thomas R. Malthus published *An Essay on the Principle of Populations,* in which he said that the passion for human reproduction is so great that if there were no checks on population growth the population would increase at a more rapid rate than its food supply. He also said that populations tend to rise to the food-carrying capacity of the environment. In the long run, he said, the power of human population growth is greater than Earth's capacity to provide the required amount of food. The result, he concluded, must be misery, disease, and starvation for vast numbers of people.

In the Near East and the Indus River Valley, controlled agriculture meant a reliable food supply, for a time at least, which encouraged population increase if it did not actually cause it. In all species, populations living in favorable environments tend to express their maximum reproductive power and grow, although that is not always so among human populations. Also, population density tends to be higher where environmental conditions are most favorable, and lower where conditions are least favorable.

Ideal environmental conditions—gentle climate, abundant food and natural resources—usually are not the rule. Nearly always there are temporary periods of drought somewhere in the world, which result in a short food supply. Or among hunter-gatherer groups there may be a temporary shortage of game. Or among industrialized nations there may be shortages of any number of natural resources: oil, grazing land, timber, copper, and so on.

When too many people—or members of any other species—try to take from the environment more than the environment can supply in order to maintain growth, they exceed the carrying capacity of the environment. Any local environment, or ecosystem, has only so much to give, and when a population demands more of the ecosystem than it can supply, then the population must move elsewhere, reduce its size, or suffer the consequences. Let's consider an example of this principle.

Imagine a population of wolves, for instance, that is just the right size to obtain food by killing only old or diseased or genetically inferior rabbits in their hunting territory. This insures a balance in numbers of each species. The wolves keep the rabbit population healthy by weeding out the less fit individuals, while the rabbit population keeps the wolf population well fed. Now imagine that the wolf population suddenly increases as a result of three new wolf packs moving into the first wolf population's territory. The increased food demands soon reduce the rabbit population so much that the wolf population faces a critical food shortage. The carrying capacity of the environment has been exceeded. Some of the wolves leave the territory, some die of starvation, and others survive, but on a near-starvation level. In short, the wolf population "crashes" as a result of requiring from the environment more than the environment can give.

With that simple lesson in population ecology, let's resume our story of human population growth by finding out what happened in the Far East and across the Pacific.

The Rise of Cities: 2

The earliest cities were . . . an exceptional form of human settlement, and their abnormality was signalized and symbolized by the wall that demarcated a primitive city's diminutive area from the vast surrounding countryside. Behind and within these physical defences, a new form of social life could, and did, take shape.

—*Arnold Toynbee*

VILLAGES AND CITIES OF CHINA

Some 750,000 years ago, almost half a million years before *Homo sapiens* evolved, hunter-gatherer groups of *Homo erectus* roamed the lands around the region of Xian, China. Located about 750 miles southeast of the Yellow Sea, Xian is backed by mountains on three sides and overlooks a vast stretch of plains that lead eastward across hundreds of miles to the sea. Providing abundant food, a good climate, and rich and varied land, the region has been occupied by human types ever since those first hunter-gatherers roamed its forests and hills.

The pattern of settlement and population growth in this fertile valley followed that of people living in the Tigris-Euphrates and Indus River Valley regions. Around 4000 B.C. a group in the Xian region settled down as farmers in the permanent village of Pan-p'o. There were about five hundred inhabitants of Pan-p'o, judging from archaeological

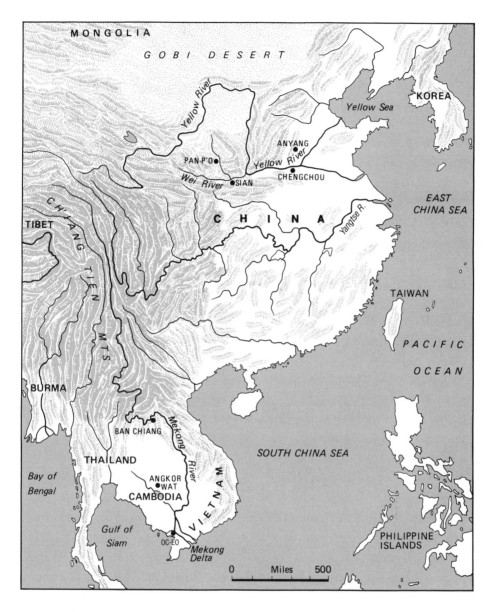

Villages established by settled farmers began to appear in northern China around 4000 B.C., about the time farming also took hold in the Indus Valley. But fishing settlements appear to have been set up as early as 8000 B.C. The first Chinese cities were built around 2000 B.C. The oldest Southeast Asian city is Vietnam's Oc-eo, which reached its peak in A.D. 220. The grandest is Cambodia's temple-city of Angko Wat, built between A.D. 1113 and 1150 by prisoners and slaves of King Suryavarman II.

How to count in Chinese

remains. These people grew millet and Chinese cabbage, had domesticated animals, fired pots in kilns, and buried their dead in a local cemetery. Some of the pottery contains twenty-two varied marks that represent numbers and probably identify the owners. Here, quite likely, was the beginning of Chinese writing, although the first scripts were not to appear until about 1400 B.C., when they were scratched into the discarded shoulder blades of oxen. Later, scribes used pens and brushes.

Pan-p'o was not an isolated village. Located near Xian on a tributary of the Wei River, it may have served as a trade center for some four hundred additional sites located in the same region and separated by a distance of a half mile to a mile from each other. The similarity in village plan among the sites suggests that still earlier groups had exchanged ideas and settled on the Pan-p'o village plan as a model to be followed. This further suggests that the time when farming and the domestication of animals began in the region was much earlier than Pan-p'o's age of 4100 B.C.

Among the evidence for still earlier settlements is pottery found in Taiwan and on the Asian mainland from as far north as Siberia to Indonesia in the south. The pottery is marked with patterns of cord and reveals the various ways in which the individual strands were arranged. Some scholars suspect that the cord was not used chiefly as a means of decorating pottery but had the more useful purpose of making fishing lines and nets. Fishing cultures, like farming cultures, imply a settled way of life. If so, then there were numerous fishing settlements in the Far East some 10,000 years ago (8000 B.C.), for that is the age of the decorated pottery.

Researchers studying the eastern plains region in northern China between the Pacific Ocean and the Wei River Valley to the west have found sickle-shaped knives, digging sticks, and other farming tools, as well as an assortment of bones of domesticated animals, including chickens, dogs, and pigs. All date between 4000 B.C. and 3000 B.C. This lowland region was swampy and ideal for growing rice. If rice farmers they were, the people who wandered onto and worked this rich land probably were immigrants in search of less crowded conditions than those of their homes in the Wei River Valley to the west. As in the Near East and later in the Indus River Valley, population pressure often forced groups to move on and settle new lands.

About a thousand years later—around 2000 B.C.—Chinese cities began to appear. The walled city of Chengchou dates to about 1600 B.C. Located on the Yellow River about three hundred miles northeast of Xian, Chengchou had surrounding satellite settlements that catered to the needs and wishes of the city's elite rulers. Artifacts recovered from these satellite workshops include arrowheads made from the bones of pigs, cattle, deer, and humans. There also were ax heads and pottery.

ANCESTOR WORSHIP AND SACRIFICE

The ancient Chinese city of Anyang tells us much about early Chinese social customs and religious beliefs around 1200 B.C. and later. Archaeologists have recovered some thirty thousand bones and other objects from Anyang since excavation began there in 1928. Some bear writing; many were "oracle bones" used in fortune telling. Most that bear writing contain messages directed to the dead, evidence that the people of Anyang believed in the religion of ancestor worship, as do many Chinese and Japanese to this day.

Ancestor worship probably began in still earlier times when a beloved grandparent or parent died and was buried in the family cemetery. At the burial of the loved one, a goat or sheep was slaughtered so that the dead ancestor would have food in the afterlife. By the time cities arose, the custom of animal sacrifice came to be practiced on a large scale in order to assure comfort in the afterlife for the ancestors of divine kings or emperors.

By 1200 B.C. humans were commonly included as sacrificial victims. We know this because the royal cemetery at Anyang contains the heads and other dismembered parts of 164 men. To celebrate the completion of one temple, more than six hundred people were killed. The sacrificing of humans probably was in part an emperor's way of letting his subjects know that he was firmly in charge and that they had better watch their step. This was carried to an extreme when armies of the Anyang period were sent on missions to round up people to serve as slaves and later be slaughtered and offered in ancestor worship sacrifice. Centuries later human sacrifice as part of religious worship was to be practiced by the Indians of Mesoamerica.

CITIES OF SOUTHEAST ASIA

Between 10,000 and 15,000 years ago people of Southeast Asia were working their tropical ecosystem for food. Like their neighbors to the north in China and to the west in the Indus River Valley, these southeast Asians had come to feel the pressure of population increases and crowding, but on a scale more serious than in the north and west. As on the coastal plains of ancient Israel and other ocean shorelines, melting glaciers in high northern latitudes had been causing a steady rise in sea level in Southeast Asia and forcing populations to retreat inland. Flooding of the coastal lands of Southeast Asia reduced the available land area to about half of what it was earlier.

Instead of practicing irrigation agriculture, the people of Southeast Asia adopted a form of agriculture called "slash and burn," which is still used in several parts of the world today. It consists of cutting and then burning a section of forest. Gardens are planted on the cleared land. When the soil becomes exhausted after a few years of intensive use, the farmers leave that land and slash and burn another area not far away. When that area becomes exhausted, they return to their earlier fields, which have recovered somewhat in the meantime.

In northern Thailand is the site of the village of Ban Chiang, which was old when Anyang was just starting. Many items have been recovered from the site, which covered about one square mile. Diggers have found burial sites, beautifully painted pottery, bronze tools, and jewelry dated at about 3600 B.C.

The oldest known city of Southeast Asia is Oc-eo in Vietnam's Mekong Delta region. A half-dozen or so bombed and looted mounds are all that is left of this city that covered 1,100 acres and has been described as a "small-scale Venice" because it once had an elaborate system of canals. A sixty-mile-long grand canal linked Oc-eo with the sea and with many smaller villages to the northeast. Chinese officials reportedly visited Oc-eo at its height in the year A.D. 220. Like centers in the Indus Valley, Oc-eo seems to have been planned, as if built according to architects' drawings. Evidence of contact with other centers far away are artifacts that include a Roman gold medal dated A.D. 152, a statue of a Hindu-style god, and rings with the early writing of India. From the time of Oc-eo, the story of social and political advances in Southeast Asia is one of increased numbers of people, power, and cities.

Just west of Vietnam in Cambodia are the remains of the most remarkable temple and city ruins in Asia, Angkor Wat. A million people once lived in this ancient city, which had hospitals staffed with doctors and nurses. Rediscovered in the mid-1800s, the great temple was built for King Suryavarman II between A.D. 1113 and 1150 by slaves and prisoners. It rivals in size and splendor the buildings of Greece and Rome and is as massive as any cathedral of Europe built during the same period. The Angkor Wat temple towers 230 feet high and covers an area of about 48,000 square yards with its three terraces and nine towers. It has an outer moat about 360 feet wide and twelve miles around.

WEST TO AFRICA

As in the Near East, India, and China, the earliest signs of agriculture in Africa can be found in a river valley whose flood waters each season enriched the land with fertile topsoil washed down onto a broad flood plain. In this case, the flood plain was the Nile River Valley.

Tushka is a site some three hundred miles west of the Red Sea along the east bank of the Nile River above the Aswan Dam. Stones used for grinding and other artifacts uncovered in the area suggest that the people living there about 15,000 years ago harvested cereal grasses as part of their diet. Other sites northward along the Nile from Tushka also show signs that wheatlike cereal grasses were harvested, grasses that may have grown wild rather than been planted. As in other regions of the world where hunter-gatherer populations thrived and multiplied, a scarcity of game due to overhunting most likely spurred a dependence on plant harvesting or cultivation from time to time. The discovery of human skeletons struck with arrowheads also suggests crowding due to population increases. Certain settled or semisettled groups must have conducted warfare from time to time to protect their land, or to encroach on their neighbors' land when food was scarce.

There also is evidence that 15,000 years ago groups along the coastal plains of North Africa had become skilled in managing herds of game animals, including Barbary sheep. Some 11,000 years ago in Syria, hunter-gatherers had learned to slaughter entire herds of Persian gazelles by driving them into large enclosure traps, called kites, when the herds migrated northward in early summer. By 6000 B.C. desert kites were common also in northern Jordan. Animal bones uncovered in the region show that from between 9000 B.C. and 6500 B.C., 80 percent of the bones were those of the Persian gazelle, and 10 percent were those of sheep and goats. The mass slaughters apparently reduced the number of gazelles severely, because after 6500 B.C. only 20 percent of the bones were those of gazelles, and more than 60 percent were those of sheep and goats. Modern hunting in the region has caused the Persian gazelle to become extinct.

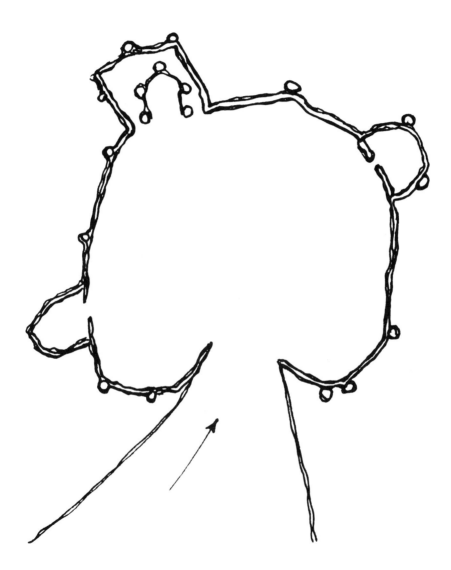

People of the Near East had become skilled at trapping large numbers of game earlier than 7000 B.C. Archaeological remains show that fenced traps, called kites, were in common use in northern Jordan to trap gazelles. The animals were driven into a wide funnel-shaped entrance to a corral enclosure that had smaller side enclosures.

As a hunter-gatherer life in northern Africa became harder and less certain, more and more people moved off the surrounding plains and into the Nile River Valley. By about 4000 B.C. controlled agriculture had taken over in North Africa as the surest means of a reliable food supply. Small villages sprang up all along the Nile from Tushka northward to the Mediterranean Sea.

By about 3500 B.C. communication among the various cultures of the Near East, Indus River Valley, and North Africa probably was common because of brisk trading among them. Trade always means a rapid exchange of ideas as well as goods. The wheel had been invented, metals were being used for tools, and boats were carrying items of trade by river and sea. The rulers of the new city-states—major cities that had their own collections of serving satellite villages—shared many concerns and must have been eager to swap ideas. They would have wanted to learn of the newest and best methods of irrigation, sources of new and better materials, and ways of best maintaining political power over their satellite villages and over the thousands of peasants who worked the land and the artisans and craftsmen who designed and built the temples.

Evidence of such communication is found in the Egyptian center of Hierakonpolis, built around 3200 B.C. on the Nile about 250 miles north of Tushka. The city's gateway is a near duplicate of those built at Uruk across the Mediterranean in Iraq some three hundred years earlier. Hierakonpolis served as the southern capital of Egypt and covered an area of more than forty acres, including a large cemetery. An estimated 5,000 to 10,000 workers lived outside the city wall in small houses of mud brick with flat roofs on which they slept during hot weather. The second, and northern, capital of Egypt was Buto, located on the Nile delta at the edge of the Mediterranean. Soon after the construction of Hierakonpolis, Upper Egypt was conquered violently by Lower Egypt and unified as the Kingdom of the Two Lands.

At about the time Hierakonpolis was being established, Egyptian writing appeared. At first, it was crude and quite limited in use, but by 3200 B.C. it had leaped forward to the advanced stage of the earlier

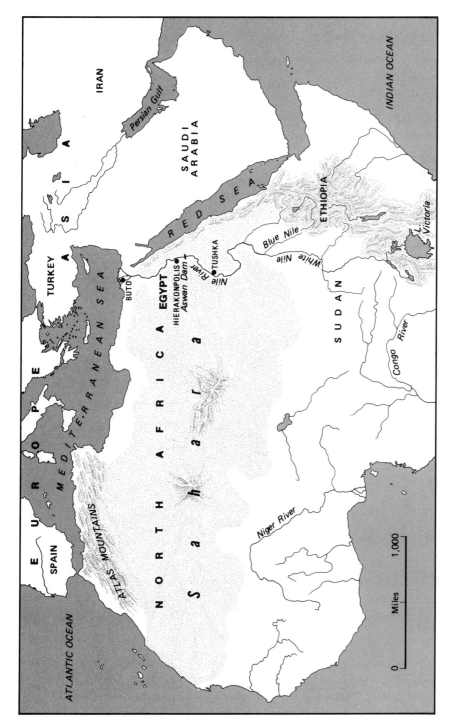

Although the original home of mankind, Africa did not give rise to the first centers of civilization. As in the Middle East and India, agriculture and the first permanent settlements took root in a rich river valley, the Nile River Valley. Tushka, just south of the Aswan Dam, was among Africa's earliest agricultural centers, some 15,000 years old.

Ancient Egyptian writing included symbols for letters of an alphabet, and signs with more general meaning. The cartouche, or name plate, for the Egyptian queen Cleopatra is shown with its alphabetic symbols. The two signs at left are "determinatives," used at the end of a text passage to indicate that the passage has something to do involving the mouth (top), such as speaking or eating; or involves the gods (bottom).

cuneiform writing of the Near East. Called hieroglyphic writing, it contained a mix of pictures representing objects, called ideograms, and signs standing for certain sounds, called phonetic signs. Both had been developed earlier in the Near East. In short, Egyptian script quickly attained a high level of efficiency, as if Egyptian intellectuals had had teachers, which they almost certainly did. But instead of doing their writing by making impressions on clay tablets, the Egyptians made paper and wrote on it with ink. Hieroglyphic writing was to remain in use for some three thousand years. Says the British archaeologist Jacquetta Hawkes, "The borrowers had quickly surpassed the inventors."

The work of Patrick Munson of Indiana University has helped piece together how climate and population growth affected people living in

How to count in Egyptian

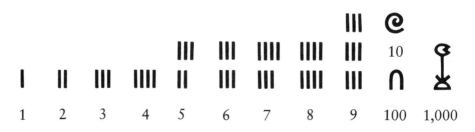

By about 3500 B.C. the Egyptians had mastered the craft of making refining metal and fashioning metal objects. Egyptian pictograms show a cartoon strip sequence first of superheating a fire with foot bellows (top), then removing a container of melted metal from the fire (bottom), and pouring it into small containers (right). At far right, a laborer empties a sack of ore crushed and ready for processing.

the region of the southwestern Sahara some four thousand and more years ago. Munson's work includes excavation of sites near old, dried-up lakes along a twenty-five-mile section of seven-hundred-foot-high cliffs that extend for some three hundred miles in central Mauritania. Remains he has dug up—including signs of hunter-gatherers, grinding stones, projectile points, engravings of cattle and wild animals of the hunt, pottery, and seed remains—have enabled him to glimpse the lives of those sub-Saharan people who lived more than four thousand years ago in villages near the old lakes and along the cliff tops.

Sometime after about 2500 B.C., and again around 1100 B.C., the pace of the drying trend that began after the last ice age seems to have quickened around the sub-Saharan region. These drying periods reduced the amount of wild game, caused first a shrinking and then a drying up of the lakes, and made grazing land for domestic herds scarcer. Meanwhile, local populations in the villages continued to grow. At first, two villages at the base of the cliffs contained from five hundred to a thousand people each. As population grew, new villages were built atop the cliffs and by about 700 B.C. their populations stood at about 10,000 people living in walled enclosures. These "forts" seem to have been designed to protect the villagers and their precious food stores from plunder by outsiders.

Continued drought conditions, coupled with population growth, made life for these people ever harder. Their herds soon overgrazed the land, and what little rain that came washed away much of the then topsoil. According to scientists who study the effects of drought and

Before 1983, soil destruction in Africa's Kenya, for example, was rapid because of a lack of land management. While population pressure forced farmers to work marginal lands such as steep slopes, overgrazing by cattle, such as sheep in this photograph, further eroded the soil. Education in land management since 1983 has helped reverse the trend of soil erosion and deforestation, but much still needs to be done.

overgrazing, the reduced plant cover changed local weather patterns by reflecting back to the atmosphere so much of the Sun's radiation that rainfall in the overgrazed areas was cut by about 40 percent. Less rain in turn meant even less plant cover. So near-drought conditions brought on periodically by nature were speeded and intensified by overgrazing. By 400 B.C. the cliff-top villages were gone and replaced by clusters of only a few shabby huts. According to Munson, it was most likely a combination of continued drought and continued raids by well-armed Berber warriors from the north that caused the population collapse of this sub-Saharan region.

Civilization grew at a slower pace in Africa south of the Equator than in the north. Not until about 500 B.C. was the shift made from stone tools and a hunter-gathering way of life to farming. To this day in many parts of southern Africa relatively isolated groups live pretty much as their hunter-gatherer ancestors of five thousand years ago did.

NORTH TO EUROPE

In Chapter 3 we left the Cro-Magnon hunter-gatherers living in southern and central Europe at the base of the glaciers of the last ice age. They lived in small groups and used caves for shelter. The ice-age beasts that roamed the forests and the open tundra provided food; their skins and bones were fashioned into tools and weapons, and used for shelter.

The retreat of the glacial ice brought a warmer and drier climate, and we might think it would have ushered in a favorable time for those Europeans, but it did not. By about 10,000 years ago the mammoths, the migratory reindeer, and other game species were gone. Artifacts left by the hunter-gatherers show that they changed from a diet of big game to one of small animals, fish, and wild plants. Rising sea levels caused by the melting glacial ice crowded groups together, which caused keen competition for food and living space. During the period of from 10,000 to 7,000 years ago, according to one estimate, the population of Europe may have fallen from about half a million to a quarter of a million.

The retreat of the great ice from northern Europe, and a more favorable climate, opened new land for settlement. A rule of nature says that when a new ecological niche is opened it is soon occupied. Gradually over centuries small and scattered bands of hunter-gatherers were replaced by groups of newcomers—settled farmers—from the Near East. Wave on wave of them packed up and moved westward, crossing Turkey, then Greece, and into Bulgaria.

Several early farming villages numbering from one hundred to three hundred people have been uncovered in Greece and Bulgaria. Certain sites in Greece reveal the sudden appearance of a complete agricultural "tool kit" of artifacts typical of skilled farmers—including sickle blades, food storage jars, tools for grinding wheat into flour, and the remains of goats, sheep, and other domesticated animals. It is as if a new people just moved in, or as if an older hunter-gatherer group had been joined and taught a new way of life.

THE PALACE AT KNOSSOS

Sometime around 6000 B.C., long before the Near Eastern city of Uruk had been built, a group of some fifty to one hundred skilled farmers from around the region that is now Turkey built boats and sailed south to the Mediterranean island of Crete, where they set up a colony complete with stores of food and a variety of domesticated animals. The village they established, known as Knossos, eventually commanded an area of some six hundred square miles and reached a population of about 50,000. Its artisans, architects, and craftsmen over the years produced one of the most elegant palaces the world has known.

Minos seems to have been the name of the first Cretan king, who began work on the palace at about the time when Uruk was being built. In his honor, each of the future kings of Crete took the name of Minos and added to the palace to suit his own taste. There were large storerooms with great jars for wine and olive oil. Some of the jars stood as tall as a man and can be seen in place today. There were also containers lined with fragments of gold leaf. These were probably from the rooms where the Minoan kings kept their stores of gold, silver, and other

Wall paintings like this one at Knossos are evidence that the Minoans engaged in a sport involving acrobats vaulting over the horns of bulls.

precious metals. Nearby were apartments of the royal guards who kept watch over the king's wealth.

The palace also had an elaborate plumbing system that was not to be equaled in all of Europe until the mid-1800s. Enormous clay pipes, some large enough for a person to stand up in, carried water and sewage away from the palace. There also was a system of pipes throughout the palace for hot and cold water. After four thousand years, the drainage system at Knossos is still in working order.

The Minoans developed a system of picture writing known as Linear A. It may have led to an early stage of writing in which symbols came to stand for sounds rather than objects. A more advanced form of syllable writing, known as Linear B and used by both the Minoans and people on the mainland, was an early form of Greek writing. Recall that writing in the Near East and later in Egypt also advanced from pictures that represented objects to pictures that represented sounds.

Knossos enjoyed its years of splendor between 2000 B.C. and 1700 B.C., around the time when cities were rising in the Indus Valley and

This example of syllabic script of the ancient Phoenicians dates from the 18th to the 15th centuries B.C.

northern China. About the year 1450 B.C. Knossos and other Minoan centers burned. By fifty years later the centers had been completely destroyed. Some scholars have thought that invaders swept over the island, but it seems more likely that a catastrophic explosion of the volcanic island of Thera, sixty miles north of Crete, sent the Minoans and their splendid civilization into oblivion.

FROM STONEHENGE TO CATHEDRALS

While the Minoan kings were reigning gloriously, an elaborate stone structure known as Stonehenge was in use in England. Built around 1850 B.C., Stonehenge has been described as a "stone-age computer," since it was used to make astronomical observations to gain information about a calendar. Consisting of six huge circles within circles, some still marked by enormous standing stones weighing several tons, it could be used to predict eclipses and mark the exact time of the changing seasons. Other massive stone structures in Europe are even older than Stonehenge. Some in France date to 4500 B.C. Others have been found in Ireland and northern Scotland. Some of the stone structures appear to be tombs that also served as gathering places for the people who built them. The early tombs were less elaborate and massive than the later one. One in Brittany took an estimated five thousand man-hours to build, whereas Stonehenge took an estimated 30 *million* man-hours.

During the heyday of Knossos, tribes of Greeks were building powerful states defended by hill fortresses. Among the richest and most powerful was Mycenae, dating from about 1600 to 1450 B.C. Its royal tombs contained beautifully fashioned gold masks, bracelets, and vases.

By 600 B.C. the Greeks ruled over two thousand square miles of coastline from Spain in the west to the Black Sea in the east. Their civilization reached its peak in the fifth century B.C. By about 400 B.C. they had a democratic form of government. About this time, and later, the Greeks had become pioneers in scientific thought, medicine, math-

A massive circular arrangement of gigantic stone slabs known as Stone-henge, in England, stands as an early "computer" for predicting astro-nomical events such as eclipses of the Sun and Moon, occurrences of the solstices and equinoxes, and a sophisticated calendar.

ematics, astronomy, drama, poetry, and philosophy. The names of many of their leading thinkers ring through history and include Thales, Socrates, Plato, Aristotle, Pythagoras, Archimedes, and many more.

Another great civilization—that of the Romans—was in the making around 500 B.C. Five hundred years earlier farmers from the lands ruled by the Greeks had settled in Italy as far south as Sicily. By 338 B.C., a powerful group in central Italy—the Romans—had defeated the many small mountain tribes of that region, and soon after came to rule all of Italy. Like the Greeks before them, the Romans were people of law and government. They also were accomplished civil engineers and masters of trade who gradually expanded their rule far from Rome.

By about 500 B.C. people known as the Celts dominated northern Europe and held that rule for five hundred years. They had tools made of iron, including saws, files, and chisels. They were traders and builders and erected western Europe's first cities, including the walled city of Bibracte in what is now eastern France. Bibracte's population of some 40,000 enjoyed a system of roads, a marketplace, and a religious center extending over some 330 acres. In 390 B.C. Celtic armies successfully invaded Greece and Italy, but in turn the Celts were defeated by Julius Caesar's Roman legions around 50 B.C., and Bibracte for a time became Caesar's headquarters.

These and other such events begin to sound familiar and play much more prominent roles in our history books than do the events so far recounted. Over the next two hundred and more years, many cities sprang up in Europe, and along with them enormous cathedrals, many of which stand today. Such massive undertakings imply rapid population growth accompanied by a rapid growth in the size of cities. Like the pyramids of Egypt, Europe's massive cathedrals required the labor of thousands of skilled workers over many years.

But before continuing our account of population growth in Europe—and the calamities that often accompanied it—we will return to Southeast Asia and take up our story of the peopling of the lands of the Pacific and the New World.

Across the Pacific to the New World

We read the past by the light of the present, and the forms vary as the shadows fall, or as the point of vision alters.

—J. A. Froude

AUSTRALIA'S FIRST SETTLERS

As we found in earlier chapters, by some 750,000 years ago *Homo erectus* types were following a hunter-gatherer way of life in parts of China and Southeast Asia. And by 50,000 years ago *Homo sapiens sapiens* had taken up life in many parts of the world, including Asia, where our story of the peopling of Australia and the many islands of the Pacific Ocean begins.

By some 40,000 or more years ago people of Southeast Asia had become expert enough with boats, rafts, and the sea to make their way island by island across the Pacific to the sprawling continent of Australia. At the time we are talking about, much of the world's free water was locked up as glacial ice so that sea level was one hundred or more feet lower than it is now. This meant that many of today's islands off the coast of Southeast Asia—including Borneo, for instance—were then part of the mainland. People could simply have walked eastward until they came to water and then done some island hopping until they arrived at what is now New Guinea. Another walk southward would have brought them onto what is now Australia, since Australia was then linked by a broad land bridge with New Guinea and with Tasmania to the south. Once begun, those early migrations from Southeast Asia to Australia must have come one after another, accompanied by waves of exploration and settlement of the major islands eastward across a large part of the Pacific. During such waves of exploration and settlement, the original Australians may have been displaced by latercomers and forced southward to Tasmania.

Some anthropologists challenge the idea that the Australian Aborigines came from Southeast Asia. They say that the Aborigines share certain similarities with some of the hill tribes of India, people who might have made the trip from southern India by sea at a time when the seas were shallower and straits narrower.

During the past twenty years, archaeologists working the area around Lake Mungo in southern Australia have turned up freshwater mussel shells, charred bones, stone tools, and human remains dated at 28,000 years old. (To find out how scientists date ancient shells, bone, and other organic remains, see Appendix, page 145.)

The 28,000-year-old Mungo Lake skeleton had the appearance of a recent person. Then workers digging an irrigation canal 150 miles south of Mungo Lake, in the Kow Swamp, uncovered about forty more skeletons whose skulls appeared very old. They had large jaws and a prominent brow ridge like that of Neanderthal people. But these older-appearing Kow Swamp skulls turned out to be younger than the modern-appearing Lake Mungo skulls. The mystery has yet to be solved, but it appears certain that some 28,000 or more years ago two distinct racial types of humans were living together in Australia. Today there is but a single aboriginal Australian stock.

What is equally puzzling is that neither of the prehistoric groups ever appears to have taken up settled farming as a way of life. At least no such evidence was at hand in Australia in the 1600s when Europeans first explored the Pacific islands. Australia was the only land that did not have settled farmers. For some reason the aboriginal groups there never made the switch from a hunter-gatherer life. Later, in 1788, when

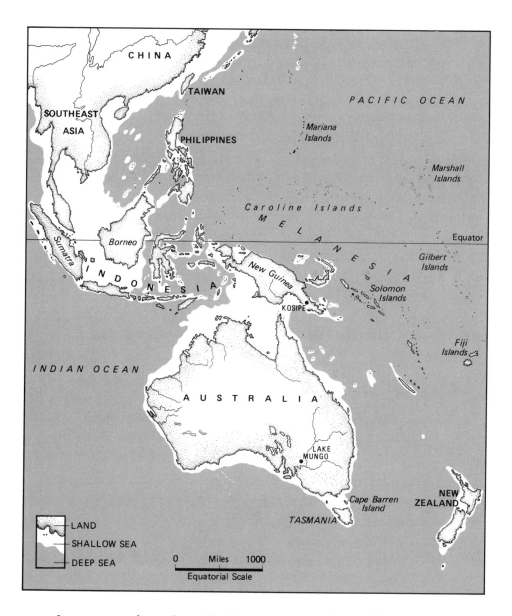

It now seems that at least 40,000 years ago peoples from Southeast Asia began to island hop their way to populate the many islands of the vast Pacific Ocean. Their route to Australia could have been southeastward across Indonesia to New Guinea. Australia, then connected to New Guinea by a land bridge when sea level was lower, would have been easily accessible. The hundreds of remote small islands could have been reached easily by boat over the following centuries.

European settlers occupied Australia, the aboriginal population was little changed, with about 300,000 inhabitants, two-thirds of whom lived in the rich tropical region along the coast of Arnhem Land and other such productive areas in the southeast.

Later still in the 1800s, according to anthropologist Ashley Montagu, successive waves of British settlers "did their best to exterminate the aborigines" in Australia and Tasmania. Many were murdered as their kangaroo hunting ranges were taken over by the British. A shortage of laborers to manage the settlers' farms and herds of sheep led the British to kidnap aboriginal children and use them as slave labor. According to anthropologist Lyndall Ryan, many aboriginal graveyards were dug up, and the bones of those buried were cut into pieces and sold to museums as specimens of "prehistoric missing links." The last full-blooded aboriginal Tasmanian, the daughter of a chief, died in 1876, and in 1904 her skeleton was hung for display in the Royal Society of Tasmania Museum. (In the 1700s and 1800s the American Indians suffered similar persecution and indignities at the hands of European settlers.)

Today about two thousand Tasmanian Aborigines remain living as outcasts on Cape Barren Island, off Tasmania's northeast coast. They are the offspring of full-blooded Tasmanian aboriginal women who bore the children of European seal hunters from 1800 to 1837.

THE SETTLEMENT OF NEW GUINEA

On New Guinea to the north is a site named Kosipe, which dates to some 25,000 years ago. The first cultivated gardens of New Guinea were worked much later, sometime around 7000 B.C., which is about the same time as early agriculture in the Near East and China. Farming methods for many New Guinea tribes changed little, if at all, over the next few thousand years. Today many pry up roots with wooden digging sticks that are exactly the same as digging sticks found in a peat bog and dated at 2,300 years.

As occurred in other parts of the world, in New Guinea population growth among hunter-gatherer groups in one valley provided the pressure for some to pack up and move on in search of less crowded regions. With fewer and fewer unspoiled hunting ranges available, a life-style change to agriculture occurred in New Guinea also. Continued population growth meant that ever more land to farm was needed. New land came by conquering your neighbors and replacing them, or by moving on. This pattern has been repeated a thousand times in a thousand different places the world over.

In general, waves of expansion eastward from the Southeast Asia mainland, especially from about 3000 B.C. to 1500 B.C. and later, gradually led to the population of the Pacific islands eastward from New Guinea to the Hawaiian Islands in the north and Polynesia in the south. The new settlers traveled in great outrigger canoes, navigating by the Sun and stars and following the flight of birds. Their baggage included pigs, chickens, dogs, coconuts, breadfruit, yams, and taro. Among their tools were hand axes, stone files, and tools made from the teeth of sharks and whales.

EAST TO THE NEW WORLD

One of the liveliest topics in anthropology today is when the peopling of the Americas took place. As elsewhere in the world, during the last ice age that gripped a large part of North America, ocean levels dropped and exposed much coastal land that is now under water. As Australia and New Guinea for a while were linked by a broad land bridge, so were Alaska and Siberia in northeast Asia. Called Beringia, that land bridge was some one thousand miles wide. At least 12,000 years ago, before the ice withdrew completely, groups of people from Siberia crossed over to what is now Alaska. They are called the Paleo-Indians (*paleo* meaning "ancient"). In only a few centuries they evolved rich cultural traditions in settlements ranging from Alaska to the southern tip of South America, and from the Pacific coast to the Atlantic.

Some paleontologists, including several associated with the Center for the Study of the First Americans of the University of Maine at Orono, think that the waves of Paleo-Indian migrations began much earlier, probably 30,000 to 50,000 years ago. According to the Center's director, Robson Bonnichsen, "For evidence we have the following: flaked mammoth bone dated greater than 30,000 years old from sites in the Old Crow Basin of the northern Yukon Territory; worked bones from El Cedral, northern Mexico, more than 33,000 years old, and a long sequence of simple flaked tools from Toca do Boqueirao da Pedra Furada, Brazil, quite likely extending back to 50,000 to 60,000 years ago."

In the summer of 1988 I visited a Paleo-Indian site in Montana being worked by Bonnichsen. At an elevation of some seven thousand feet amid the dry rolling grasslands of southwestern Montana, the site over the past several seasons has yielded several thousand tools flaked from stone called chert or made of antler bone. Geologic evidence revealed a few weeks before my arrival at the site makes Bonnichsen and his geologist colleagues suspect that the site had been occupied by Paleo-Indians possibly as early as 50,000 years ago. But such an ancient date has yet to be confirmed.

The first major civilization in the New World was that of the Olmecs, established in what is today southern Mexico in 1250 B.C., some eight hundred years after the earliest Chinese cities began to appear. By the year A.D. 300, Teotihuacan in Central Mexico could boast a population of 200,000 people and was the largest cultural center in the New World. Its Pyramid of the Sun was larger than the great Egyptian pyramids at Giza, built some three thousand years earlier.

As Teotihuacan slipped into decline, to the south the Mayan culture, which had begun around 500 B.C., flowered and came to dominate the land for a thousand years. Cities such as Uxmal, Chichén Itzá, Tikal, and Copan became important centers bustling with trade and producing splendid works of art. Tikal's population probably was about 40,000. In all, about sixty Mayan cities have been identified in present regions of the Yucatan Peninsula, Guatemala, Belize, and southernmost Mexico, an area larger than that formed by the New England states. Several of the local populations were organized into city-states that regularly

Paleo-Indian sites, such as this one being excavated by the Center for the Study of the First Americans, and examined by the author in southwestern Montana in 1988, abound in North America. The earth from carefully dug pits, precisely marked off with string grids, is sifted by the teaspoonful for remains that might have been fashioned by humans.

Flint-knapper with a knack, Dr. Robson Bonnichsen, Director of the Center for the Study of the First Americans, fashions a projectile point of chert from the same stone quarry used by Paleo-Indians more than 10,000 years ago. By carefully studying such ancient tools, archaeologists can deduce how a certain tool was made and then duplicate it.

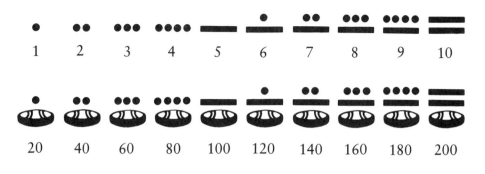

How to count in Maya

warred with each other, as was true earlier among the Babylonian city-states and later elsewhere. At its peak, between A.D. 700 and A.D. 800, the Mayan civilization probably numbered 5 million people.

In North America over the following centuries, thousands of Indian villages large and small dotted the landscape eastward to the Atlantic Ocean, but none grew to the size of the Central American city-states or achieved their architectural splendor or their mastery over religious and political affairs.

In the extreme northwest were the Eskimos and Aleuts, who settled that region only some six thousand or so years ago. Earlier arrivals had populated all of the United States and southern Canada much earlier. Among them were Indians of the Northwest Coast, who included the Nootka, Haida, Coola, Tlingit, and Chinook. In the Southwest were other groups belonging to three cultural provinces. The two major ones were the Anasazi and the Hohokam. The third is the Mogollon. All were confined to the regions of Colorado, Utah, Nevada, Arizona, and New Mexico. The Anasazi reached their cultural peak between A.D. 900 and 1100. They carved their presence in New Mexico's ten-mile-long Chaco Canyon by constructing eight major apartment-building complexes called pueblos.

Plains Indians sprawled over a huge area extending from Texas to Canada, and from the Mississippi River to the Rocky Mountains. While Indians of the western plains were wanderers and lived in temporary shelters, those of the eastern plains were more settled. The Mandan, for instance, built huge earth lodges supported by thick beams and covered with sod. Hundreds of tribes lived on the great plains—including the Kansa, Omaha, Iowa, Missouri, Hidatsa, Ponca, Osage, Wichita, Apache, and Kiowa.

Among the tribes in the area of what is now New England were the Micmac, Abenaki, and Narragansett, for example, who lived in small villages in wigwams, domed structures covered with animal skins and bark that were supported by young trees. They found rich resources in the sea—mussels and clams, crabs, lobsters, and sea bass—and hunted wild game and gathered edible plants.

New York's tribes belonged to five "nations"—the Cayuga, Seneca, Onondaga, Mohawk, and Oneida—that were collectively known as the Iroquois. Their dwellings and settlements were larger than those of the tribes to the north and east. Instead of wigwams, they lived in clusters

Betalakin House remains of stone blocks date to around A.D. *1000 and are typical of many such dwellings made by Indians of the Southwest. These remains are part of New Mexico's Navajo National Monument.*

of large (from one hundred to three hundred feet long) houses of logs enclosed within a protective stockade. The population of such a community may have numbered a few hundred. Without access to the rich food source of the sea, the Iroquois depended on farming more than the coastal tribes did.

Around the Great Lakes and south into West Virginia were the tribes Miami, Kickapoo, Winnebago, and Shawnee, among others. They were less settled than the Iroquois, practicing farming on only a limited scale and depending largely on a hunting-gathering existence.

Because these tribes of the Northeast were frequently fighting and raiding each other, trade among them posed certain dangers. The Iroquois were especially warlike, attacking neighboring Iroquoian groups and groups of the Algonquian tribes. It is not clear whether they carried out their raids to expand their territories and so acquire more land for farming, or for other reasons. In any case, population pressure most likely was the root cause.

By about A.D. 1500, wars among the five tribes of the Iroquois had become so common that the tribal chiefs met and called a truce. The resulting union of tribes gave them much-needed strength against the waves of European settlers in the 1600s and 1700s, but by the late 1700s the size of the Iroquois tribes had been greatly reduced. The arrows and clubs of the Indians were no match for the guns of the Europeans. Also new diseases brought by the Europeans killed the Indians off by the thousands since they had no natural defenses against them. In many cases those who were not killed in battle or by disease were simply driven westward, off their land. The Europeans had an advanced technology with highly efficient tools of iron. Whenever the two cultures clashed, the Indians were greatly outpaced technologically, and as a result their future was bleak.

What had happened back on the European continent from the time Julius Caesar's legions had marched from Rome and defeated the Celts in Western Europe? One thing was inescapable. European cultures had advanced at a dizzying rate and were flexing their technological and cultural muscles wherever they could.

Europe's Population Growth to 1850

To be ignorant of what happened before you were born is to be ever a child. For what is the value of human life unless it is interwoven with past events by the records of history?
—*Marcus Tullius Cicero*

EUROPE'S DARK AGES

As surely as great cities rise and blaze brightly for a while, they one day crumble to dust, and where they once stood new cities rise. None of the great centers—Uruk, Ur, Mohenjo-Daro, Harappa, Angkor Wat, Knossos, Teotihuacan—lasted long, and today they clink to the tune of the archaeologist's spade. As the Roman philosopher-poet Lucretius said, "No single thing abides."

That was true also of the great centers of learning and government that became the classical worlds of Greece and Rome. But lust for power and war, spawned by people pressure, crushed those worlds also. The time after the Roman Empire fell is sometimes called the Dark Ages in Europe and spans the period from A.D. 500 to 1000.

Sometime before A.D. 500, there were an estimated 300 million people in the world. Among them were the savage Tartar-Mongolian warriors, who had fought their way across Central Asia into Europe and had begun to attack the numerous groups of central and northern Europeans who still lived largely by hunting and primitive farming.

These European groups were organized into tribal units that included the Goths, Visigoths, Vandals, Franks, Burgundians, Angles, Saxons, and Jutes. Although they spoke a common language, few individuals among them could read or write.

The European tribes long had been envious of the warm lands around the Mediterranean that were part of the Roman Empire. But until A.D. 500 Roman armies had managed to keep them under control. Now that the European tribes themselves were being attacked and forced from their lands by the Tartar-Mongolians, they stepped up their attacks on the Romans and eventually defeated them. By A.D. 455 Rome had been captured twice, once by the Visigoths and once by the Vandals. Within fifty years, the whole western Roman Empire had been splintered into several Germanic kingdoms ruled by warring chiefs.

The next five hundred years were times of great hardship for the growing population of Europe. In the absence of Roman law, warriors were free to loot for profit and to kill for food with little worry of punishment. Continued fear of attack caused many towns to erect defensive walls, such as York in England and Florence in Italy. Trade declined, and with fewer markets available, fewer goods were made and less food was grown. As food supplies dwindled, the artisans, builders, and shopkeepers in the towns began to feel the pinch of hunger. Only those who farmed had an assured supply of food. Europe's major cities shrank, including Cologne in Germany, Lyons in France, and London in England. In Rome itself, the population dwindled from about a million to only 50,000 or so.

While Europe was gripped by hardship during the years from A.D. 500 to 1000, to the east in the Islamic center of Bagdad, culture and learning flowered under the Arabs. In A.D. 830, for instance, the Caliph al-Mamun set up a House of Wisdom. Moslem scholars translated thousands of old Greek scientific, medical, philosophical, and mathematical works into Arabic and so preserved them. In this way the Arabs mastered a great body of learning that had been begun long ago by the Babylonians and later taken over and improved on by the Greeks. In addition, the Moslems carried on brisk trade in luxuries unknown to the Europeans. Islamic trade routes laced major centers from Spain in the west, at that time a Moslem stronghold, to China in the east and deep into Africa as far south as Timbuktu.

THE MIDDLE AGES

The period known as the Middle Ages, which spans the years from about 1000 to 1400, marked a time of renewed growth in Europe. Villages again grew into towns and towns into cities, and a lively rebirth of trade linked previously isolated villages with the great cultural centers to the east and south. The main cause of this wave of cultural activity was the peace that followed two hundred years of war (the Crusades, in the eleventh, twelfth, and thirteenth centuries) between Moslem and Christian armies. During that time contact with the Moslems had exposed Europeans to many Eastern luxuries including spices, sugar, rugs, and tapestries. Once peace had been restored, a European appetite for those luxuries sparked a lively trade. From Moslem strongholds along the East African coast, for example, jewelry and fine carvings of gold, ivory, and clear quartz crystal found eager buyers in the European marketplace.

During the four centuries of the Middle Ages European artisans, influenced by exposure to Moslem luxuries, wove beautiful tapestries and produced thousands of fine paintings and works of sculpture. As the power of the Roman Catholic church grew, Latin, the language of the Church, became the language of scholars and the elite throughout Europe. Students from faraway lands came to the many large universities that sprang up. Magnificent new cathedrals stretched skyward and dominated their towns, as they do to this day in such places as Chartres in France, Ulm in Germany, and Salisbury in England.

Wherever new trade routes were opened or old ones reopened, Roman Catholic missionaries followed on the heels of the traders to win converts to the Church. The Church had become an international power from Norway in the north to Sicily in the south. The European kings of the Middle Ages, many of them descended from chiefs of the

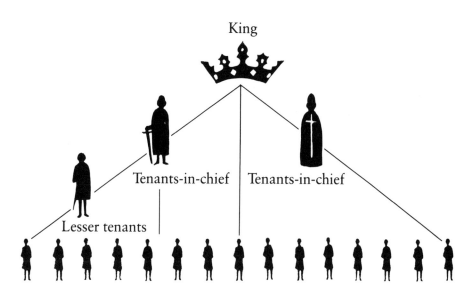

King

Tenants-in-chief | Tenants-in-chief

Lesser tenants

During the Middle Ages society was highly structured. At the top were the kings, many of them former chiefs of barbarian tribes, of the many small European "states." Beneath the kings were tenants-in-chief, who ruled over lesser tenants, who directed peasants who worked the land.

earlier European tribes, resented the Church's interference in their local pockets of power. The kings wanted their subjects to be loyal to them, not to the Church leaders in Rome. Such competition between kings and popes, with the kings struggling to keep the loyalty of their people, paved the way for the establishment of strong local governments, which grew into the early separate nation-states of Europe.

YEARS OF THE BLACK DEATH

As we have seen in this and earlier chapters, during times of local or regional hardship brought on by overcrowding, drought, war, or decline in trade, many local populations shrink as artisans, craftsmen, and others die or leave a crowded region to take up life elsewhere. A grim example is the period during the Middle Ages when bubonic plague—known as the "Black Death"—swept through Europe.

The first reported outbreak of plague, around the year 500, killed an estimated 100 million people out of a total world population of an estimated 150 million. Plague was transmitted by fleas carried by black rats and certain other rodents. Although there had been outbreaks of plague earlier, none had been as severe as the one that hit Europe in 1348. It seems to have started in the ports of Italy and swept across Spain, France, England, central Europe and Scandinavia over the next two years. In one three-year period from 1348 through 1350 plague killed one out of every four people in Europe. Over the next fifty years more outbreaks killed off one-third of Europe's population.

The disease struck swiftly, killing its victims within five or six days. Bubonic plague begins with a high fever, then red blotches appear on the body and turn dark, during which time the stricken person goes through agonizing pain before collapsing. The innocent-sounding nursery song "Ring around the rosie, pocket full of posie, one, two, three, we all fall down" was sung by children at that time. The "ring around the rosie" referred to the inflamed red spot; the "posie" carried in the pocket was a medicinal plant that was supposed to ward off illness; and "one, two, three, we all fall down" meant that people with the telltale inflammation would soon start dropping like flies.

Plague struck rich and poor alike but was especially bad in areas with poor sanitation and high population density. It peaked in the summer months when fleas were most plentiful. It tapered off in winter, only to increase again in the spring. And it returned in cycles of about ten years. London was struck by the disease twenty times during the 1400s; Venice was hit twenty-three times between 1348 and 1576. The death toll of plague victims at various times in three Italian and one French city tells its own story:

THE EFFECT OF PLAGUE ON POPULATION

City	Pre-plague Population	Deaths
Florence	90,000	45,000
Siena	42,000	27,000
Venice	160,000	46,721
Marseilles	90,000	40,000

The Black Death struck Europe many times over the centuries. It was especially severe in the 1300s, sometimes claiming one out of every three or four people. Had a Gallup poll of Europeans been taken then, most would have claimed that "the end of the world" was taking place.

From 1348 to 1374 plague reduced England's population from about 3.8 million to 2.1 million. Western and central Europe were struck so hard that it took almost two hundred years for the population to return to the preplague level. Spain was among the worst-hit, losing half a million of its inhabitants over the six-year period from 1596 to 1602. Outbreaks later in the century claimed another half million. According to historian William McNeill, plague "must be considered as one of the significant factors in Spain's decline as an economic and political power" in the later 1600s.

It is hard to imagine the terror people must have felt, not knowing what caused the disease, knowing there was no cure for it, and helplessly watching friends and loved ones toppling around them. As we found in Chapter 1, people create myths to explain away the mysterious and so provide at least some comfort during mental anguish. Over the plague years, superstition, rumor, belief in witchcraft, and religion all provided false hope and wild explanations for the dying.

In some areas the Jews were blamed for the outbreaks, accused of poisoning public water supplies. In France, physicians were stoned in the streets, accused of spreading the plague at the direction of the rich in order to kill off the large population of poor people. The members of a religious cult known as the flagellants paraded through many of the streets of Europe, whipping each other and warning those at hand to rid themselves of their sins. Christians flocked to the churches pleading for protection by the Virgin Mary, Saint Sebastian, and scores of other saints. But in many cases the priests had fled the cities for the relative safety of the country and left their churches empty. Most believed that the deaths were the work of God, punishment for mankind's sins.

The plague years provide valuable insights into human nature in the face of widespread disaster. How do people behave during such times of stress? And did they behave any differently during the fourteenth century from the way we behave today? Most people then panicked and ran for safety. Those who could afford to fled the cities and took refuge in the country, where there were fewer people. Some turned to the Church, offering whatever wealth they had and vowing to lead lives of righteousness should they be spared the dreaded disease. Others made the best of what little time they might have left. Liquor flowed more freely than ever, moral standards collapsed, and the general attitude was one of self-indulgence. "Eat, drink, and be merry, for tomorrow we may die," was the frame of mind.

If husbands and wives suspected each other of having the disease, they deserted each other. Mothers abandoned their stricken children. Many of the terrified committed suicide rather than risk facing an agonizing death. Armed troops surrounded afflicted sections of a city, or a whole town, permitting no one to leave or enter under the penalty of death. Gallows were erected in public squares just as reminders. Gravediggers were, understandably, hard to find and commanded a high price. Thieves, murderers, and the insane often did the job, sometimes not bothering to distinguish between the dead and the dying, indiscriminately dumping the bodies into large open graves after stealing whatever they could.

Whenever the plague all but disappeared, as suddenly and as often as it had in the past, people moved back to the cities and tried to pick up their lives as before, but a great cloud of gloom hung over all of Europe.

For some, the plague years had been profitable, since they inherited land and wealth from plague-stricken relatives. But for the farmers, fewer people in the cities meant a reduced market for crops. Some gave up working the land and moved to the cities themselves, finding employment as artisans, craftsmen, and builders.

Europe was not alone in losing large parts of its population through plague. A combination of war and disease cut down China's population from 123 million to a mere 65 million between the years 1200 and 1393.

WARS AND POPULATION CHANGE

As disease epidemics bring temporary changes in local populations, so do wars. Population pressure, religion, politics, and lust for power are the principal causes of war.

Some societies loved war for its own sake, the Maoris of New Zealand, the Zulus of southern Africa, and the Scandinavian Norsemen, among them. The Norse view of heaven was a place where one could engage in battle for eternity, where wounds healed immediately and the "dead" could rise to fight again, endlessly.

Wars began as small affairs, quarrels between local rulers, but as local populations grew so did the armies. Population growth and technological advances have combined to assure that the number of victims in each new major war exceeds that of the previous one. For example, some 10 million fighting troops were killed during World War I compared with nearly 17 million in World War II, or 20 million including civilians.

From 1550 to 1650 wars raged through Europe. The armies of Europe's numerous nation-states were frequently at each other's throats, and for three decades from 1618 to 1648 European Protestants fought Catholics in what became known as the Thirty Years' War. Possibly as many as one-third of the inhabitants of Germany and Bohemia were slaughtered, and in one crushing attack on Magdeburg by Catholic forces in 1631 an estimated 20,000 people were killed.

During times of war, birth rates usually decline while death rates increase, resulting in a short-term population loss. In the Middle Ages and later, the Swiss controlled their population growth by carrying on a lively business in mercenary soldiers, hiring out their young men to the armies of other countries. In 1748 there was a total of about 40,000 Swiss mercenaries in the service of France and Holland. Many failed to return and start families. During the 1700s Switzerland lost about half a million of its 1.5 million population on the battlefields.

Throughout the Middle Ages and later, disease occurred most often in military encampments and along trade routes, where population densities were high and sanitary conditions were poor. Recall that Malthus said that disease was one of the three checks on population growth. Chief among the population-reducing diseases were tuberculosis, typhus, smallpox, and two varieties of the plague. Before 1800 wherever smallpox struck, out of every hundred people only four escaped the disease, which was fatal in one out of five cases and accounted for 10 percent of all deaths. Around 1760 the mathematician Daniel Bernouille calculated that a world average of 600,000 people died of smallpox each year. In Russia two million lives were lost to smallpox in a single year.

EUROPE'S 200-YEAR POPULATION BOOM

In Europe, the years from 1650 to about 1750 saw rapid population growth. Plague had disappeared and the times were relatively peaceful. Improvements in crops and farming techniques were making food more plentiful; the discovery that clover renewed the soil meant that more land could be kept under cultivation. In this period, also, many Europeans left to settle in North America, which reduced population density on the land and so encouraged population growth.

From 1650 to 1750, Europe's population soared, the combined populations of Russia and Europe leaping by 40 million. By 1750 the world population had grown to about 800 million. (Although it is hard to account for, the population of Asia also jumped by some 50 to 75 percent during that hundred-year period.) Over the next century to 1850 Europe's population doubled! Many saw cause for concern in this rapid rise, and a host of legal, social, and cultural restraints were brought into play. Few of these restraints were humane by today's standards. For example, large landowners controlled their local populations by approving or denying permission for their serfs and other workers to marry. They also could refuse to build additional cottages to house new families. Most governments also imposed marriage restrictions, aimed mainly at the poor in order to prevent welfare cases from mushrooming. In England the New Poor Law of 1834 segregated all males and females admitted to public workhouses, including married couples. The craft unions joined in by requiring young men to undergo a long period of training before they could marry.

The most effective of the checks on population growth during this period was the murder, either direct or through abandonment, of infants and young children. In England and in many parts of the Continent, dead infants lying in the streets or on trash heaps were a common sight. The poor simply were unable to feed the large numbers of legitimate and illegitimate children they were producing.

Many who found the growing rate of infant murder shocking started homes, called foundling homes, to care for unwanted children. Unhappily, the move caused more misery than help. Thomas Coram, a retired English sea captain, opened a foundling home in 1741 with financial support from the government. By the entrance gate was a basket with a bell so that a mother could leave her infant in the dead of night, ring the bell to signal that an infant had been left, and then depart in secrecy. Fifteen thousand infants were accepted in the first four years, of whom 10,600 died of malnutrition and related ailments due to lack of women to breast feed the infants. In county parish foundling homes conditions were so bad that more than 95 percent of the infants died.

In France the number of abandoned infants increased from about 40,000 in 1784 to 138,000 in 1822. In Paris alone, infants were being abandoned at the rate of about 6,500 a year. French foundling homes met the same fate as those in England. There were not enough women to nurse the infants, with the result that 80 percent of the infants died within their first year. Another 10 percent or more died soon after, even though as much as one-half of the nation's income was used to support state foundling homes.

In addition to improved agriculture's effect on promoting population growth, in 1798 Edward Jenner produced a vaccine against smallpox, which significantly reduced the high number of deaths from the disease. In England alone the death rate from smallpox fell from about 3,500 people out of every million in the 1700s to only 90 per million after 1872. Advances in medical treatment coupled with improved sanitary conditions in cities and towns also reduced deaths and so caused rapid population growth.

By 1850 the world population had swollen to 1 billion.

THE POTATO AND IRELAND'S POPULATION CRASH

Around 1750, farmers in North America had begun to export to Europe an abundance of two highly nutritious crops—potatoes and corn. These new-to-Europe food plants produced a 30 percent increase in food supply for Europe's people, including its huge population of poor people. What happened to Ireland's population as a result of the lowly potato holds an important ecological lesson. It also is an interesting case history for Malthus's prediction that a population will increase to the level of its ability to produce food.

Until the mid-1700s, the Irish had grown and relied on cereals as their chief crop, but then they discovered the potato on importing it from America. So successful was it as a source of food that the Irish all but abandoned their cereal crops and became a one-crop nation, relying on the potato. Over the years to about 1840, the Irish became affluent and began to raise large families and marry at an earlier age than before. As their food source became plentiful and reliable, the Irish watched their population grow by leaps and bounds. But then in the 1840s a disastrous failure of the potato crop occurred for several successive years and widespread famine followed. Before the famine, Ireland's population had doubled to about 8 million. During and just after the famine the population dropped dramatically to 5 million. About 1 million had died, while another 2 million had left the country for Europe or North America. Stunned by the experience, the remaining 5 million did not overpopulate again and did not return to a single-crop system of agriculture.

The Irish developed a variety of farming practices, including raising beef cattle and manufacturing dairy products. Although a significant part of the population chose not to marry at all, the portion that did marry married late and had smaller families, practices that have continued to this day. In 1960, for example, 70 percent of Ireland's men age 25 to 34 were unmarried.

FAMINES AROUND THE WORLD

Famine is unknown in the rich nations of the world, but severe food shortages that kill millions of people through starvation have occurred many times through history, and they are bound to occur more often as the world population soars.

In 1878, Cornelius Walford compiled a list of 350 famines and wrote a thumbnail description of some of them. A selection of a few of the famines he recorded follows. Quotation marks in his chronicle indicate direct quotes from his sources.

436 B.C.   Rome: Famine. Thousands threw themselves into the Tiber [River].

A.D. 192   Ireland: General scarcity; bad harvest; mortality and emigration, "so the lands and houses, territories and tribes were emptied."

695–700   England and Ireland: Famine and pestilence during three years "so that men ate each other."

1193–1196   England and France: "Famine occasioned by incessant rains. The common people perished everywhere for lack of food."

1600   Russia: Famine and plague of which 500,000 die.

1769–1770   India (Hindustan): First great Indian famine of which we have a record. It was estimated that 3 million people perished. The air was so infected by the noxious effluvia of dead bodies that it was scarcely possible to stir abroad without perceiving it; and without hearing also the frantic cries of victims of famine who were seen at every stage of suffering and death.

1770   Bohemia: Famine and pestilence said to carry off 168,000 persons.

1790   India: Famine in district of Barda . . . so great was the distress that many people fled to other districts in search of food; while others destroyed themselves, and some killed their children and lived on their flesh.

1877–1878   North China: "Appalling famine raging throughout four provinces [of] North China. Nine million people reported destitute, children daily sold in markets for [raising means to procure] food. . . . Total population of districts affected, 70 million. . . ." The people's faces are black with hunger; they are dying by thousands upon thousands. Women and girls and boys are openly offered for sale to any chance wayfarer. When I left the country, a respectable married woman could be easily bought for six dollars, and a little girl for two. In cases, however, where it was found impossible to dispose of their children, parents have been known to kill them sooner than witness their prolonged suffering, in many instances throwing themselves afterwards down wells, or committing suicide by arsenic.

1878   Morocco: "... If you could see the terrible scenes of misery—poor starving mothers breaking and pounding up bones they find in the streets, and giving them to their famished children—it would make your heart ache."

Europe's plague years up to 1800 brings us to the edge of modern times and a renewed intensity of world population growth. Because of a lack of information, little can be said about population growth from the 1600s into the 1800s in Africa, Asia, and South America. Africa, for instance, may have stayed close to 100 million until the early 1800s. But then after the mid-1800s, European influence in Africa became strong, and Europe's technological and medical know-how began to significantly lower the African death rate. Between 1850 and 1900 Africa's population jumped some 20 to 40 percent. By 1950 it had doubled to 200 million, and by mid-1989 it had soared to 646 million. With a present growth rate that doubles its numbers every twenty-four years, Africa's population is expected to explode to 1.5 billion by the year 2020!

We are now getting into numbers whose significance can be appreciated only with at least some knowledge of terms such as birth rate, death rate, fertility, and others used by demographers, the people who specialize in the vital statistics of populations.

People and Numbers

*Man is being dwarfed by his apparatus and
stifled by his numbers, and this heavy physical
pressure on the individual is inflicting a severe
psychic distress.*

—Arnold Toynbee

RATES OF POPULATION GROWTH

Despite local temporary setbacks, the world's human population has
kept increasing ever since *Homo sapiens* arrived on the scene. Between
69 billion and 110 billion human beings have lived since *Homo sapiens*
evolved. Not only has the size of the world population increased con-

RATES OF POPULATION INCREASE

Date	Estimated World Population	Doubling Time
8000 B.C.	5 million	1,500 years
A.D. 1650	0.5 billion	200 years
1850	1 billion	80 years
1925	2 billion	45 years
1986	5 billion	40 years
2100	10 billion	(?) 15 years

tinually, but the *rate* of increase also has continued. A look at the numbers in the chart on the preceding page will make the point. "Doubling time" in the table means the length of time it takes for the world population to double.

Doubling times, of course, vary from one country to another. Doubling time assumes a constant rate of natural growth, and should not be used as a prediction of population growth. For instance, the present doubling time for Kenya is only 17 years, compared with Brazil, which is 34 years, India 32 years, China 49 years, the United States 98 years. But these figures should not be used to forecast that Brazil's 1989 population of 147 million, for example, will double to 294 million by the year 2023.

The following example makes the point of population growth rate.

HOUSEFLY REPRODUCTION FOR SEVEN GENERATIONS

Generation	Number of Parents	Number of Offspring	Total Population
1	2	120	122
2	122	7,320	7,442
3	7,442	446,520	453,962
4	453,962	27,237,720	27,691,682
5	27,691,682	1,661,500,920	1,689,192,602
6	1,689,192,602	101,351,556,120	103,040,748,722
7	103,040,748,722	6,182,444,923,320	6,285,485,672,042

A female housefly produces about 120 eggs at a time, of which about half develop into male flies and half into females. Seven generations of houseflies are produced in one year. Now let's suppose that the following very unlikely event occurred. Two houseflies mate and give rise to the remaining six generations, of which every fly born lives a full life. Also suppose that every female in her turn produces 120 eggs, each of which develops into a healthy fly. As the table shows, at the end of the seventh generation there would be more than 6 quadrillion houseflies.

Houseflies are extremely fast breeders. Elephants are the slowest breeders of all living animals. About twenty months must pass between the time a female elephant's egg is fertilized and a baby elephant is born. In comparison, it takes a human being nine months to develop from a fertilized egg to a newborn. But even at the elephant's slow rate of breeding, a lot of elephants would be around if all the females had as many healthy young as they were able to and all the young survived. Darwin worked it out roughly, based on the number of elephants living more than a hundred years ago. He said that in about 750 years there would be about 19 million elephants.

In nature, however, not every female member of a given species lives to be old enough to bear offspring, and among those who do live long enough not all have offspring, or they have offspring some of whom do not survive, or in the case of humans they may choose to have only one or two children rather than many.

In the late 1800s, about 80 percent of the women in industrialized countries were living through their peak childbearing years. This was not so of women during the previous century and earlier, when only one out of every three daughters survived long enough to have children of her own.

BIRTH RATES AND DEATH RATES

In human populations the actual birth rate never reaches the potential birth rate, as it did in the example of houseflies. In other words, although a woman is theoretically capable of bearing one child a year through her reproductive years, few do. In some parts of the world, however, large families are the rule, as in the African nation of Mauritania, where married women want an average of 9 children per family! Not surprisingly, Mauritania's population is growing very fast. Over the next several years we can expect Mauritania's death rate—now twice that of the world average of 10 out of 1,000—to lower and its (1989) life expectancy of only 45 years to rise, both of which will make the country's population grow even more rapidly than it is growing today. The increase will be due to increased medical, nutritional, and technological aid from industrialized nations.

Birth rates usually are expressed as the number of births per thousand people. For example, the 1989 birth rate for the United States was 16 babies for every 1,000 people. Since the United States population in 1989 was 249 million people, a birth rate of 16 babies per 1,000 people would amount to 3,984,000 new babies that year.

Fertility rate is another important number to know when we want to compare population growth rate trends. It is defined as the number of births per 1,000 females age 15 through 49. Fertility rate figures are more informative about population growth rate trends than birth rates because they include the population of females of reproductive age (15 to 49) only rather than the total population. "Fertility" in the table is given as "total fertility rate," the average number of children a woman can be expected to have during her child-bearing years. A total fertility rate between 2.1 and 2.5 is called the "replacement level" for a population, and it means that eventually the population will stop growing if the total fertility rate remains between 2.1 and 2.5 and the death rate remains stable.

Like birth rate, death rate can be measured as the number of deaths per 1,000 people in a population. Death rates are higher in a population with a relatively large number of old people than they are in a population with a relatively small number of old people.

A comparison of population growth rate data for the selected parts of the world represented on the next page will quickly show which regions are adding the greatest numbers of people. (Figures are based on *1989 World Population Data Sheet,* Population Reference Bureau.)

SELECTED WORLD POPULATION FIGURES, 1989

Place	Population (millions) 1989	Birth Rate	Death Rate	Doubling Time (years)	Fertility	Population (Estimate) Year 2020 (millions)
U.S.	249	16	9	98	1.9	294
China	1,104	21	7	49	2.4	1,523
India	835	33	11	32	4.3	1,376
Africa	646	45	15	24	6.3	1,523
Europe	499	13	10	269	1.7	502
S.E. Asia	445	31	9	31	3.8	740
S. America	438	29	7	33	3.6	705
U.S.S.R.	289	20	10	70	2.5	355
WORLD	5,234	28	10	39	3.6	8,330

AGE STRUCTURE AND POPULATION GROWTH RATE

Age structure is simply the percentage of people in different age groups in a population. If we want to know how rapidly a population is growing, we must know the birth rate, death rate, the rate at which people are moving into or out of the population, and the population's age structure.

We can group women into three major age classes: (1) individuals too young to have children; (2) those of an age who can have children; and (3) those too old to produce children.

THREE MAJOR AGE GROUPS OF WOMEN

Prereproductive	Reproductive	Postreproductive
Age 0–15	Age 15–49	Age 49 and over

A handy way to find out how rapidly or slowly this or that nation's population is growing is to construct an age pyramid for the nation in question. All we need to know is the percentages of the population broken down into age groups. Study the shapes of the three age pyramids in the diagram. The one at the left, with a broad base made up of prereproductive children, is typical of a population that is growing fast, such as those of Africa, India, Southeast Asia, and South America. That is because each new generation is larger than the generation of its parents.

The age pyramid in the middle is typical of a population that tends to stay pretty much the same, such as those of the United Kingdom, Austria, Greece, and Belgium. Notice the narrower base of prereproductive individuals, which means that each new generation tends to number about the same as its parent generation. The age pyramid on the right is typical of a population that is becoming smaller, such as that of Sweden. In a dwindling population each new generation is smaller than its parent generation.

Any nation that has a broad base of children under age 15, as most unindustrialized, or so-called Third World, countries do, may be headed for serious population problems, including economic and social ills, due

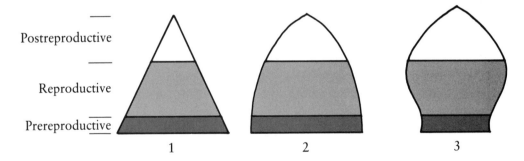

A population's growth rate is revealed by how many individuals make up its age groups based on reproductive ability. A fast-growing population (1) has a broad base of prereproductive individuals. More or less stable populations (2) have fewer prereproductive and more postreproductive individuals. A decreasing population (3) has a narrow base and large top.

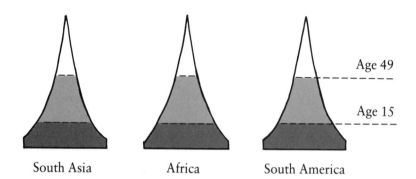

Age 49

Age 15

South Asia   Africa   South America

These three age pyramids are typical of a rapidly growing population. Forty percent of each region's individuals are below age 15, while 45 percent are in the reproductive age group (15 to 49). Data from Population Reference Bureau Bulletin, Vol. 21, No. 4, Oct. 1965.

to their explosive growth rate. As the children grow and move up into the reproductive age group, the number of females able to have children rises dramatically. In turn, their children keep broadening the base of the age pyramid still more.

As population ecologist Paul R. Erhlich and his wife Anne write,

Age pyramids of a diminishing population, characteristic of Sweden, lose population under age 15 and gain population in the postreproductive age group (over age 49). Notice the lopsided shape of these age pyramids for the years 1950 and 2000, due to the difference in male (left of center line) and female numbers in a given age group. Data from Population Reference Bureau Bulletin, Vol. 35, No. 2, June 1980.

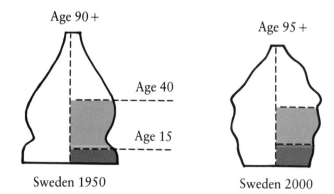

Age 90 +

Age 95 +

Age 40

Age 15

Sweden 1950   Sweden 2000

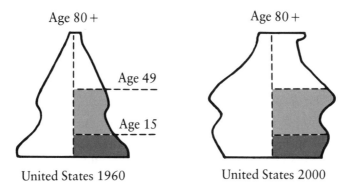

Age 80+   Age 80+

Age 49

Age 15

United States 1960   United States 2000

Age pyramids for the United States for the years 1960 and 2000 show a dramatic change in shape as the prereproductive group loses population slightly while the reproductive and postreproductive groups expand significantly. The noticeable difference in the number of males and females beginning about upper middle age is due to life expectancy of females being greater. Data for the pyramids are from Population Reference Bureau Bulletin, *Vol. 37, No. 2, June 1982.*

"These masses of young people in the [Third World countries] are the gunpowder of the population explosion. Their existence means that, even if great progress were made immediately in reducing the number of births per female in those countries, it would be some 30 years before such birth control could significantly slow population growth." Of the human population increase of 3.2 billion over the next 35 years, 95 percent will be in Third World countries.

It is the age structure of a population that shapes its growth curve. As we continue to improve infant survival through medicine, sanitation, and nutrition—even without a change in world population birth rate—the base of the age pyramid grows broader. Since medicine, sanitation, and nutrition promote longer life as well, the proportion of older people in a population also increases. The "problems" at the upper and bottom ends of an age pyramid are different in many ways and similar in others.

When we talk about population growth we must consider the role played by increasing numbers of elderly people. Around 500 B.C. a person could expect to live for 30 years on the average. By the year 1900, life had become better for many people, due to better medical care and a better diet, and life expectancy at that time was from 45 to 50 years. Today, the life expectancy is 70 or more years in developed countries. Some biologists feel that the upper age limit for humans may climb to 100 or 110 years. Because more and more people are living to an increasingly older age, the total population is expanding at the top of the age pyramid as well as at the bottom. Not only will an increasing number of the elderly have to be accommodated in industrial nations, but there must be an accompanying increase in social services to care for them.

Virtually all nations on the planet are increasing their populations, the Third World countries more rapidly than the rest. The numbers cannot be argued with. At this time our world population is increasing at a rate of 1.8 percent, or about 94 million new people, a year. That is like adding about four times the population of California or more than the population of northern Europe, each year. It can be broken down into an average increase of 260,000 people a day, or 10,750 people an hour, or about 180 people a minute. Each time your heart beats, two new people are added to the planet.

If humans had been increasing at the 1989 annual rate of 1.8 percent since the time of Christ, there would be more than 20 million people for each person now on Earth—or a grand total of 20 million times 5 billion!

That means there would be more than one hundred people for each square foot of surface of the planet! Almost a billion of the world's present population were born after 1970, and between 4 and 7 percent of all the people who have ever lived are alive today.

THE HUMAN POPULATION GROWTH CURVE

It took early humans more than a million years to increase their numbers to 1 billion by about 1850. Then it took only seventy-five years to double that number to 2 billion by 1925. By 1962, when only thirty-seven additional years had passed, we had increased the world population by still another billion, to 3 billion. By 1977, over a period of fifteen years, the population had increased still another billion to 4 billion. And by 1989, over a period of only twelve years this time, we had added *more* than a billion.

How long can this accelerating growth rate go on before we hear shouts of, "Stand back, here come the people!"? But there will be no place to stand back because someone else will already be standing there.

Like the example of a rapidly growing housefly population, our human population increase is on what demographers call a "sigmoid" (meaning S-shape) growth curve. In all biology, no known population of animals or plants has ever remained for long on the steep part of a sigmoid growth curve. Three things can happen: (1) the population curve can flatten out and continue on in a steady state with little or no total change in numbers (called "zero population growth") and be more or less in tune with the carrying capacity of the environment; (2) it can

POPULATION GROWTH CURVE

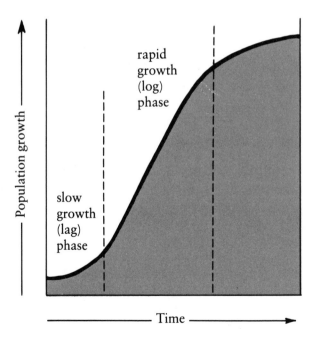

No known population has remained for long on the log phase (rapid growth phase) of a sigmoid growth curve. Such a rapidly growing population levels off and maintains a steady state, or it declines slowly, or it crashes by decreasing abruptly.

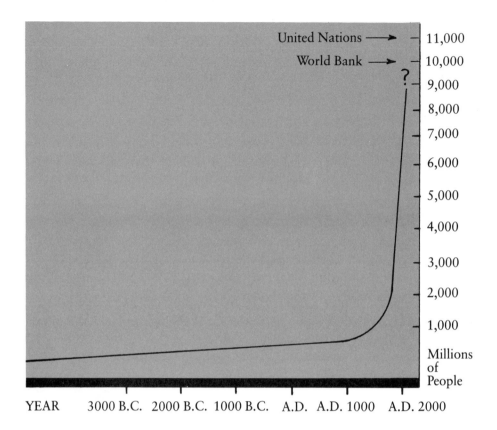

					United Nations ⟶	— 11,000
					World Bank ⟶	— 10,000
					?	— 9,000

YEAR   3000 B.C.   2000 B.C.   1000 B.C.   A.D.   A.D. 1000   A.D. 2000

The world's human population grew slowly from 3000 B.C. until relatively modern times. Its present runaway growth is viewed with alarm by many scientists. No one knows when it will stop growing and level off, or crash. The World Bank projects a peak number of 10 billion around 2090. The United Nations projects 11 billion around 2125.

decline gradually either as a result of self-imposed control (in the case of human beings) or as a result of overtaxing the resources of the environment and destroying it with overwhelming amounts of pollutants; or (3) the population can decrease rapidly, but temporarily, as a result of short-term epidemic disease, agents such as the AIDS virus, wars, famine, lack of enough environmental resources, all detonating a population crash. What is in store for our runaway human population is presently unknown, but continued rapid growth well into the next century now appears virtually unavoidable.

POPULATION CRASH CURVE

If the world population continued to double about three times a century without letup, within two centuries there would be so many people that our numbers most likely would exceed the carrying capacity of the environment. We could then expect a population crash due to widespread famine, disease caused by excessive pollution, psychological stress brought on by overcrowding or other social pressures, and murders on a small scale and wars on a large scale as people competed for possession of the remaining dwindling resources.

The process of denuding the planet of its resources would also result in widespread destruction of other species. Such a drastic loss of other species would probably bring about a severe change in ecological balance, which would further reduce the carrying capacity of the environment and hasten the crash.

ZERO POPULATION GROWTH

Another possibility, in theory at least, is for the world population voluntarily to achieve zero population growth, become stable, and continue in harmony with the environment. If we do not achieve zero population growth voluntarily, then natural forces are bound to impose it on us eventually. In brief, zero population growth means stopping population increase by bringing into the world only enough babies to replace the people who die, and maintaining that 1:1 ratio. As of 1989, Austria, East Germany, West Germany, Hungary, Italy, and Denmark were the only nations to balance their birth and death rates. Other countries that had come very close to doing so included Finland, Norway, Sweden, the United Kingdom, Belgium, Luxembourg, Bulgaria, Czechoslovakia, and Greece.

In June, 1965, then President Lyndon B. Johnson told a United Nations gathering, "Let us all in all our lands . . . including this land . . . face forthrightly the multiplying problems of our multiplying populations and seek the answers to this most profound challenge to the future of all the world. Let us act on the fact that five dollars invested in population control is worth one hundred dollars invested in economic growth." The speech was ahead of its times and its important message failed to move many listeners.

Achieving a stable world population by planning cannot come about until the world's major leaders recognize that there *is* a world population problem, adopt a population growth rate policy, and design education programs leading to voluntary regulation of the population. To date, no nation has adopted as a goal a reduction of its population growth rate. But that is no small task since a number of cultural, social, and political attitudes would have to be changed; for example, Mauritania and many other African nations have deep-rooted traditions of large families. The Malaysian government even wants to increase its country's population from 17 million in 1988 to 70 million as quickly as possible. A number of Third World nations erroneously believe that the only way to achieve economic growth is to *increase* their populations.

The attitude of organized religion also must be considered. All major Western religious groups have approved the use of birth control devices and educational programs, except for the Roman Catholic church, which continues to encourage its followers to "be fruitful and multiply." The Catholic church enjoys widespread influence over one-sixth of the world population and continually reminds its followers that it is "sinful" to use contraceptive devices as a part of family planning. This outdated attitude angers some Catholic church leaders, among them Catholic biologist John H. Thomas, who has said that "the Church must affirm that the birth rate must soon be brought in line with the death rate [to achieve a growth rate of zero] . . . and that it is time that the Church stop being like a reluctant little child, always needing to be dragged into the present." The birth rate of Latin America, a strongly Roman Catholic region, is 29 per 1,000, in fourth place after Africa, India, and Southeast Asia. The birth rate for developed nations is 15 per 1,000 people.

In the absence of any agreed-on goal among nations to contain world population, the world's number of people can only continue to skyrocket. Future rapid growth comes from the fact that about 40 percent of the population in most Third World countries is below age 15 and is the Ehrlichs' "gunpowder" for the population explosion to come.

As you found earlier, the world population is estimated to reach 8 billion by the year 2020. And present estimates put the population in the year 2100 at 10 billion people. Can the planet support that many—or more—people in ecological harmony and at a desirable level of health and the "good life?" Will people be able to manage their large numbers politically, socially, and economically to avoid any number of people-related disasters? Those are important unknowns.

THE "MODIFIED IRISH CURVE"

Still another possibility in our scenario of uncontrollably adding more and more people to the planet is the modified Irish curve, named after the potato famine in Ireland in the 1840s. One or more agrarian countries could similarly undergo devastating years of crop failures that would trigger widespread famines. Emigration, however, would not be the solution this time, as it was for large numbers of the Irish, since there would be few desirable uncrowded places left in the world. Furthermore, those countries that did have available space and resources would most likely want to keep them for themselves. According to Paul Ehrlich, it may take a series of such disasters to convince governments collectively that world population must be controlled in a thinking way rather than be allowed to run wild.

POPULATION GROWTH TRENDS TODAY

Although population growth is bound to increase in virtually all countries, it has slowed significantly in the more developed countries, including many in Europe and North America, Japan, Australia, and New Zealand, for example. Sweden actually is losing population. Since 1950 about 85 percent of world population growth has been in the Third World countries, including Africa, India, and South America. But over the past ten years birth rates and total fertility rates have lowered, if only slightly, in some of those countries. For instance, India's birth rate dropped from 39.9 in 1975 to 33 in 1989; Africa's from 46 to 45; South America's from 36.9 to 29. Birth rates also have dropped somewhat in Mexico, Thailand, and Indonesia. Some population experts anticipate that if such trends continue, a more or less steady-state world population of some 10 billion might be achieved around the year 2100.

All discussions about world population growth must have as their focus planet Earth's carrying capacity. In the United States today our politicians and economists tell us that we must steer a course of unlimited economic growth, which means creating more and more goods, together with the wastes that they produce. Raw sewage, spent medical supplies, and chemical wastes end up in our oceans and on our beaches. Deadly and long-lived radioactive wastes, which we don't know what to do with, pollute the air and drinking water, where they will remain dangerous for hundreds and thousands of years.

The idea of unlimited growth is noticeably out of step with the practice of good ecology, which recognizes that there is only a limited amount of farm and grazing land, and of space in general, on Earth; that there are limits to the land's ability to be worked and the sea's ability to provide food and serve as a world dumping ground; and that we cannot continue to strip the planet of its tropical forests, which are the most productive ecosystems on Earth.

On both the national and world levels the problem of population growth has become a matter of public policy debate, with much of the discussion focusing on regulation. In the last chapter we will return to a consideration of how human population growth might be regulated. The problems are interesting and in some ways unexpected. But now let's turn our attention to the effects of a runaway world population on Earth's resources.

CHAPTER ◇ TEN

Food and Energy
for Future Growth

*If the only check on growth of population is
starvation and misery, then any technological
improvement will have the ultimate effect of
increasing the sum of human misery as it permits a larger proportion to live in precisely the
same state of misery and starvation as before
the change.*

—*Kenneth Boulding*

DESERTS ON THE SPRAWL

Out of control, deserts in Africa, Asia, Australia, and the Americas are
spreading outward and overrunning productive farmland and grazing
land. As a result of overgrazing, woodcutting, and soil erosion, Africa's
Sahara has sprawled southward some 60 miles between 1960 and 1977.
This costly biological march has been caused in part in the central Sudan
by the number of livestock increasing about sixfold since 1957 and
overtaxing the grasses and shrubs. Northern Africa also has been hard
hit by an astronomical rise in population there since 1900.

In many parts of the world today, the picture is little changed from
three thousand and more years ago when irrigation farming in several
parts of the world exhausted and poisoned the land by causing a salt
buildup in the soil and water. Some six thousand years ago the Sumerian
culture is said to have declined as a result of salt buildup in its water

and farmland. About 15 percent of today's world population struggles to make a living from overworked farmland and grazing ranges, the quality of which continues to deteriorate. Each year millions give up the difficult battle to get food from the land and flock to overcrowded cities to compete for food and unskilled jobs. Often the areas they leave are in the early stages of becoming desert land.

"Desertification" is a term coined to describe deserts on the sprawl. Africa is not alone in witnessing the drying up of its productive land by soil erosion and desertification, which reduces the amount of land available for both grazing and farming. The Americas are being hit also—in Argentina, Brazil, large parts of Mexico, and the southwestern United States. Again, the causes are overgrazing or soil erosion and, in many regions, the massive destruction of forests by ranching corporations and land-hungry farmers.

According to Robert Repetto of the World Resources Institute of Washington, D.C., writing in the *Population Reference Bureau Bulletin* for July, 1987, "In Guatemala, 40 percent of the productive capacity of the land has been lost through erosion. In Turkey, 54 percent of the arable area is severely or very severely affected. In Mexico, roughly two-thirds of the land is moderately, severely, or totally eroded. The Food and Agricultural Organization has estimated for all developing countries that, unless effectively checked, erosion will cost 20 percent of potential agricultural production by the end of this century."

The huge Navajo Indian Reservation in northern Arizona and New Mexico provides one of the most dramatic examples of desertification from overgrazing. In the 1800s the Navajos were encouraged by the U.S. government to take up sheep farming, which they did but without a knowledge of good land management. As the sheep multiplied, the land paid a costly price. What were lush meadows carpeted with grass, mile after endless mile, in the mid-1800s today are dusty, sagebrush-dotted wasteland. As recently as the mid-1970s, a region that could support 16,000 sheep was being asked to support 11,500 Navajo people and 140,000 sheep. Proper management of that land, according to range managers, could increase its carrying capacity tenfold.

North Africa seems to have remained pretty much the same over the past one hundred years, as it has over the Middle East for the past five thousand years.

What is certain is that droughts come and go, and they are bound to continue to do so. What seems just as certain is that an increasing number of people overtaxing the land in marginal desert conditions today will soon edge that land into real desert conditions.

DROUGHT AND THE HUMAN CONDITION

In Africa, from 1968 through 1973, and then again in the 1980s, drought conditions gripped that narrow band known as the Sahel that borders the Sahara and includes Mauritania, Senegal, Mali, and Niger, in addition to Chad and Burkina Faso (formerly Upper Volta). The

Periodic drought in Ethiopia often sets the stage for mass starvation and lines of people waiting for food distributed by the International Red Cross. Many people in this January 1988 line, hopeful for their monthly ration of 35 pounds of wheat, flour, beans, and vegetable oil, have walked 30 miles, hoping that food would be waiting for them.

Dust storms, due to poor land management, regularly sweep over the Kassala district in Africa's Sudan. Here, a girl stands beside her "home" in a refugee camp. In 1985, 65,000 people lived in the camp, with 150 new families arriving every day from Eritrea and Tigrea in Ethiopia. Malnutrition and disease are common in this and other camps.

But even with controlled grazing, the world's grasslands are markedly deteriorating under growing grazing pressures. According to Robert Repetto, "at least 80 percent of African, Asian, and Middle Eastern rangelands are now assessed as moderately to severely desertified."

Is it human activity or climate change that brings on desertification? Or is it a combination of the two? Those are hard questions to answer. We know too little about the history of weather trends in most of the world's desert regions to point a finger at climate change as a cause. While some climatologists think that desertification is being aided by climate change today, others say no, pointing out that rainfall over drought of the early 1970s probably took more lives through starvation in Ethiopia than in the six Sahelian countries combined. Those seven nations have a total population of more than 78 million. Their average total fertility rate is 6.6 compared with the world average of 3.6.

In 1972 news about the great drought and famine in the Sahel caught the world's attention and sympathy. Our daily newspapers and weekly newsmagazines printed photographs of the hollow faces and matchstick limbs of starving children that haunted us. They were mostly from Chad and Burkina Faso. Sympathetic and shocked nations sent food and medical relief to the stricken areas. According to Erik Eckholm, director of the Worldwatch Institute, "proud nomads never before so humbled poured into relief camps and West Africa's cities. And still there were deaths—perhaps a hundred thousand."

Two, three, or four consecutive years of widespread drought in a region with a large population are bound to cause hundreds of thousands to millions of deaths from starvation and related diseases. The humanitarian response in such a situation is for the rich nations of the world to send food and medical supplies to aid the stricken population and keep as many people as possible alive. But what are the long-term effects of such a humanitarian gesture? There are two sides to the coin of this problem, and both sides should be considered carefully for short-term "benefits" and long-term effects.

Suppose that we are dealing with a country that has more people than it can grow food for, which includes several African nations, for example. Even in the best of times the country has to import much or most of its food. Further suppose that the country's birth rate and total fertility rate are nearly double that of the world average, and that the death rate is only slightly above the world average. In other words, this is a country whose population is growing very rapidly; each year its population increases by 15 million, as has happened in India.

Next, suppose that three successive years of drought grip the country and a cry for help goes out. Some of the rich nations respond and send enough of their surplus grain to feed the starving millions. The next year those benefactor nations will have to send grain again, plus

The Ethiopian drought of 1984 painfully drew the life out of many suffering from malnutrition. This child, his face "aged" by starvation, is so weak that he can barely hold his milk bowl. During 1984 the UN/ FAO World Food Program supplied some 60 million dollars worth of emergency food to Ethiopia. Future drought will claim more lives.

enough more to feed an additional 15 million; and the following year they will have to send that amount plus still more to feed *another* additional 15 million. The following year the drought breaks and the farmers return to working the land. Since most of the cattle have died of starvation, what was once grazing land can now be used as additional farmland. But even this additional farmland would not have been enough to feed the numbers of people before the drought and certainly cannot feed the additional 45 million that now exist. So the country is faced with importing much more food than it can pay for, and the surplus crops of the rich nations have been so drained that these nations are no longer able to help. With too little surplus food, they risk facing a shortage themselves should drought strike them next year. What to do?

So a humanitarian act has turned into a nightmare. Is the idea to "share and share alike" realistic in view of the fact that today the world's total food supply is inadequate to feed all the world's people at an acceptable nutritional standard set by the United Nations Food and Agriculture Organization (FAO)? Is the solution to the world's food problem to deplete the rich nations' surplus food stores in order to save starving millions in drought years—or even during normal times—so that those millions may survive to produce an even larger population that will require even more food, and so on and so on until the population crashes?

According to World Bank estimates, more than one-sixth of the world's population now lives in absolute poverty, barely able to survive. About 500 million people suffer from malnutrition, which is caused by not having enough food or getting too little of one or more essential nutrients such as protein, calcium, or vitamin C. Further, on a worldwide basis, deaths due to malnutrition of children under age five number about 10 million a year. In India alone a million children die each year from malnutrition.

On a global basis 12,000 people die of starvation each day. Those are the deaths we seldom hear about. It seems that unless a "media event" is made of such conditions no one much cares.

"MIRACLE" RICE: MYTH OR REALITY?

Until the early 1960s, when most nations needed more food they opened up new farmlands. That situation is no longer true. Since that time cropland area has grown relatively slowly while the emphasis has been placed on increasing the amount of food that can be produced from the same amount of land. This has been accomplished by the high use of fertilizers, pesticides, and new plant varieties in an effort called the "green revolution." Among the results were new strains of high-yield "miracle rice" and "miracle wheat," crops which at best filled many mouths temporarily while the population continued to grow. And that temporary relief came at a terrible cost.

First of all, high technology agriculture meant irrigation. Extensive irrigation without adequate drainage, which is expensive, spells trouble after a while. A poorly drained irrigation system causes a buildup of salts in the water bathing the root-zone level of the crops. When too many salts collect, the yield of a crop is reduced and eventually destroyed.

High technology agriculture also meant the use of huge amounts of fertilizers, pesticides, machinery, and the pollution they cause. And in many areas old storage and transportation systems had to be replaced, at great expense. In 1981 in India, for example, it cost more than 5 billion dollars each year for fertilizer, pesticides, and agricultural equipment to feed that nation's people at a bare self-sufficiency level.

Widespread use of pesticides has posed some especially interesting problems. The pesticides worked well enough for a while, but then many of the insect pests they were supposed to control evolved immunity to the poisons. Humans, however, have not developed immunity, with the result that the World Health Organization estimates that hundreds of thousands of people die each year from acute pesticide poisoning.

Still another problem of the "green revolution" is the risk of putting all our plant genes in one basket. As the many genetically different types of rice and wheat are replaced with only a few genetic varieties, those fewer varieties are more vulnerable to the many plant diseases and insect pests. For example, in 1946 a new, and single, oat variety was planted on 30 million acres of U.S. land. The new variety, called "Victoria type," was hailed as being resistant to a plant disease known as rust, but it did not have the genetic mixture of traditional oat seeds. All went well for the first two years. Then a new plant disease struck and wiped out the Victoria type, which had only a limited genetic defense. It disappeared almost overnight from those 30 million acres.

The "miracle rice" and "miracle wheat" varieties at best may be temporary measures, not long-term solutions to feeding a world population that is running out of control. Furthermore, a number of "miracle" grains have proved to be poor in protein content. All such measures can do is buy a little time before the next tidal wave of people comes crashing down on the environment.

But what about the longer-term future, over the next century or more? Feeding so many people may take the use of all available cropland worked with the greatest efficiency, coupled with the skill of genetic engineers.

Most population ecologists feel that the ultimate solution must be population control. According to climatologist Reid A. Bryson, "The alternative to these times of mass starvation and death is to keep population near or below the number that can be supported in the *worst* of times, not in the best of times and not even in 'average' times."

A population expert in India has remarked that most of his upper-class countrymen "would be perfectly happy to see fifty percent of the lower class Indian population disappear," so rapidly is that nation's population of 835 million growing with a doubling time of only thirty two years. In 1975, India's Minister of Agriculture told a concerned world press that his country's famines and the deaths resulting from them "ought to be thought a blessing rather than a curse."

EARTH'S RENEWABLE RESOURCES

Growth in industrial activity, in response to growth in population, is disturbing Earth's natural systems in many ways, some that we are aware of and most likely others that we are unaware of.

Natural resources include those that are renewable and those that are not renewable. Renewable resources include land, water, and the plants and animals with which we share Earth's ecosystems. As new croplands are opened up and old ones are paved over with highways, parking lots, and developments, the parts of the ecosystem that must supply lumber and other materials suffer, but they are not destroyed forever, only for as long as human activity manages to subdue them. Among those resources are vast stretches of tropical forests and their inhabitants. In Madagascar, for example, some 60,000 species of plants and animals have become extinct as a result of 93 percent of the island's eastern forest being stripped. According to Robert Repetto, "tens of thousands of species must have been eliminated" as a result of the stripping of forests in western Ecuador.

In Brazil people in overpopulated regions have cut millions of acres of rain forest, supposing that the cleared land would be suitable for farming, which it is not. People in some regions are beginning to see the dangers of forest destruction. Flooding caused by massive deforestation has recently caused Thailand to ban all logging operations, and Malaysia is considering doing the same.

Like tropical forests, marshlands are highly productive biologically. In the past 150 years, as vast stretches of marshes have been drained for farming and developments, between 25 to 50 percent of the world's marshlands have been lost.

Not too long ago the American grasslands supported herds of millions of bison, elk, and antelope. Virtually all are now gone, and the animals living on Africa's grasslands are presently meeting the same fate. Those that are left, including elephants, are mostly confined to parks and preserves, where they are easy prey for poachers. Poachers have been largely responsible for reducing Africa's elephant population of 1.2 million ten years ago to fewer than 650,000 in 1989. Prized for their horns, more than three quarters of Africa's black rhinoceros population has been wiped out by poachers since 1980.

As we take increasingly large amounts of copper, coal, uranium, and other materials from Earth's thin crust of rock, we leave the unmistakable and ugly scars of our human handiwork. The scale of land destruction caused by open pit mining must be seen to be realized. The electrical power line barely visible at top left in this photograph of an open pit copper mine in Butte, Montana, gives some idea of scale. The unnatural blue-green color of the stagnant and toxic lake left by the mining operation adds to the other-worldly character of the scene.

EARTH'S NONRENEWABLE RESOURCES

The developed nations and the newly developing ones depend on numerous nonrenewable resources, including fossil fuels (coal, oil, and gas) and metals. These resources are said to be "nonrenewable" because the geologic processes that form them take thousands or hundreds of thousands of years. Industry gobbles up the planet's nonrenewable resources at an ever increasing rate. Since 1900 aluminum production has increased 1,700-fold, petroleum production 125-fold, steel production 70-fold, and coal production 7-fold.

Does this mean that we can soon expect to run out of one or more of these resources? That question is hard to answer. If we ask whether we are in danger of running out of the stores of copper, aluminum, coal, and other resources locked up in Earth's crustal rock, the answer probably is no, with a few exceptions. But if we ask whether we can keep digging or pumping those resources out of the ground over the next century or more at an affordable cost, that is another matter. The deeper we have to dig or drill for a resource, the more expensive it becomes. If it turns out that the cost of mining a resource, such as copper, is more than people can afford to pay for the copper, then the answer is that we have *effectively* run out of that resource. Mineral "reserves" depend on a knowledge of the existence of a given mineral, the availability of the technology to mine it, and the cost of mining it. According to Robert Repetto, at present it appears that "important" metals, including iron, aluminum, and manganese, exist in adequate supply at a manageable cost indefinitely.

A growing population needs a growing amount of energy to light and heat its homes and power its factories. Today there seems to be enough economically recoverable coal to last at least a few centuries. The availability of petroleum and natural gas over the next century is less certain. Some experts say that we will begin to feel an oil and natural gas squeeze in from twenty to forty years. The high prices of oil imposed by the mostly Arab nations of the Organization of Petroleum Exporting Countries (OPEC) in the early 1970s encouraged exploration for oil in Mexico, the North Sea, and elsewhere, so that by 1985 the Arab nations were selling the rest of the world just over half as much oil as they did in 1974. There was, and continues to be, less dependency on oil and more on natural gas, coal, and hydroelectricity. Reliance on oil for commercial energy dropped from 46 percent in 1974 to about 38 percent in 1985.

As Third World countries manage to cross the line from less developed to more developed nations and raise their living standards, their people will come to expect a fair share of the good life. That will mean great new demands on energy to supply the materials, goods, and services presently enjoyed by developed countries of the Western world. At present no one can predict what mammoth additional stresses this will place on the environment. One thing seems clear, however: If the Third World countries try to improve their condition by using the methods pioneered by the rich nations, the result will be ecological disaster.

Let us now ask the final, and perhaps most important, question about the relentless march of the human population into the future. How will our runaway world population affect the quality of life?

Population and the Quality of Life

Year after year ... additional land is converted to waste by humans, who are in many cases forced to compromise their futures by circumstances beyond their control.
—Erik Eckholm and Lester R. Brown

A SEARCH FOR OPTIMUM POPULATION SIZE

Population ecologist Paul Ehrlich has said that "the idea of controlling the size of the human population is really a new one," and that attempts to limit population have been regarded as impossible or improper. As Ehrlich further points out, "that the human population is now putting stress upon the carrying capacity of Earth itself must be recognized by all responsible people, not just by ecologists. . . . It is unmistakably clear that the time has come for humanity to take a careful look at its resources, its ideals, and its numbers, and try to make some serious judgments about optimum population size, both for individual countries and for the world as a whole."

When population ecologists say that a region is "overcrowded," what do they mean? About five hundred African Bushmen need about 5,000 square miles of land for their hunting-gathering way of life and for shelter. Add another five hundred people to their vast range and the area would be "overcrowded." When we say that a region is overcrowded, we must consider two things—the number of people in relation to the available resources that the environment can supply, and the impact on the environment imposed by the disposal of wastes. Both add up to the quality of life. It is that view of "crowding" that we will examine in this chapter.

THE VANISHING OZONE LAYER

Every time an old refrigerator is crushed for junk, or you press the button of an aerosol can of hair spray, fly killer, or whipped cream, a substance known as Freon is released into the air. Freon belongs to a class of chemicals known as halocarbons, which contain the gas chlorine (Cl). And every time one of the giant supersonic passenger planes cruises through the stratosphere it releases quantities of the chemical nitric oxide (NO), which is one atom of nitrogen bonded to one atom of oxygen.

Both the chlorine and the nitric oxide find their way into that layer of gases in the stratosphere called the ozone layer. Ozone is a special form of oxygen having three (O_3) instead of two (O_2) atoms, and the ozone layer provides a natural protective shield against the high-energy ultraviolet radiation from the Sun. Without the ozone layer, we humans would run a higher risk of getting skin cancer and damaging our immune systems; agricultural crop yields would suffer, touching off famines; larval forms of some marine life would be destroyed; and a slight warming of the atmosphere would begin.

Another group of chemicals are the chlorofluorocarbons. The two most common are $CFCl_3$, widely used as a propellant in aerosol spray cans in much of Europe, but banned in the United States, Canada, Norway, and Sweden in the 1970s, and Freon (CF_2Cl_2). Once they enter the atmosphere, $CFCl_3$ has a lifetime of 64 years and Freon a lifetime of 108 years. Eventually, both gases are carried aloft into the stratosphere where, broken down by ultraviolet radiation, they release their chlorine. The free chlorine then attacks and breaks down ozone into ordinary oxygen. Other CFCs are widely used in polyurethane foam seat cushions, building insulation, and as agents for metal cleaning, sterilization of medical equipment, and fast freezing of foods.

Nitric oxide released by the supersonic transports also breaks down ozone. First, the nitric oxide combines with ozone and breaks it down to nitrogen dioxide (NO_2) and oxygen (O_2). Next, the nitrogen dioxide combines with an oxygen atom and produces more nitric oxide (NO) plus oxygen (O_2). The new nitric oxide is then available to break down more ozone and so continue the cycle.

According to an international group of more than one hundred experts, between 1978 and 1985 the amount of stratospheric ozone had dropped by 2.5 percent as a result of human pollution and natural causes, which include solar activity, volcanoes, and upper atmosphere wind patterns. According to the National Academy of Sciences, a 1 percent drop in the ozone layer causes a 2 to 6 percent increase in skin cancer rates. The ozone layer may eventually decrease by 5 to 9 percent. That could mean an additional 43,000 cases of skin cancer each year in the United States alone. According to the Environmental Protection Agency (EPA), if nations do not agree to cut down on the use of CFCs, an estimated 3 million people either alive today or born before 2075 may be killed by exposure to ultraviolet radiation. Ozone loss has been greatest over the polar regions and least over midlatitudes. Even so, ozone loss over the mid–Northern Hemisphere was between 1.7 and 3 percent from 1970 to 1988.

Another ozone destroyer is the gas nitrous oxide (N_2O), which is being produced in ever larger amounts by the increased use of nitrogen fertilizers. Those who look to technological miracles to save the starving millions occupying arid lands of the globe advocate limitless use of nitrogen fertilizers to increase crop yields. It is projected that the use of this industrially produced fertilizer will increase by hundreds of percent over the next twenty-five or so years.

Destruction of Earth's ozone layer, according to a report of the National Research Council (NRC), increases the threat of "drastic" climate changes. According to Veerauhadran Ramanathan of the National Aeronautics and Space Administration (NASA), the halocarbons and chlorofluorocarbons (CFCs) that attack ozone also absorb long-wave (heat) radiation reflected by Earth's surface and so tend to produce a "greenhouse effect," as do carbon dioxide (CO_2), water vapor, and certain other gases. (The glass of a greenhouse permits the passage of short-wave radiation from the Sun into the greenhouse but traps the long-wave, or heat, radiation reradiated from the ground and plants within the greenhouse.) The NRC report estimated that the effect produced by these "greenhouse gases" might contribute a global temperature increase of at least 0.5°C over a fifty-year period. While 0.5°C may not seem like much of a temperature rise, it is significant on a global scale. Other sources forecast an even sharper rise, from 1.5 to 4.5°C, according to the World Resources Institute.

The warning of danger to the ozone layer was first sounded by chemists Sherwood Rowland and Mario Molina of the University of California, Irvine in 1974, but some members of the scientific community were skeptical of just how serious the danger might be. As the debate continued, industry took advantage of it and continued to produce more and more CFCs. Then in 1985 scientists discovered a leak in the ozone layer over Antarctica, a gaping hole as large as the United States and whose size varies with the seasons. It is now certain, according to atmospheric chemist James Anderson of Harvard University, that "there would be no ozone hole without CFCs."

Can anything be done to stop the destruction to the ozone layer? The only ways are to greatly reduce or stop the use of the harmful agents by finding other, harmless chemicals to take their place. And the news appears promising, if uncertain. In September, 1987, thirty-four nations, including the United States, signed a treaty to protect the ozone layer by reducing CFC production 35 to 50 percent by the year 2000.

Nature's healing of the ozone layer might be a slow process. Some experts feel that the high levels of chlorine in the air now will remain until the twenty-second century, and possibly longer. Once in the stratosphere, a single chlorine atom can destroy 10,000 ozone molecules. To show the seriousness of the problem, even if CFC emissions were cut by 85 percent right now, the present ozone-hungry chlorine level probably would not drop for decades. And if CFCs were banned completely tomorrow, because of the long life of CFCs it might take one hundred years to regain the ozone already lost.

We simply do not know to what extent the world's industrial giants may have permanently damaged the fragile ozone layer that protects all living things. Says atmospheric physicist Michael Oppenheimer of the Environmental Defense Fund, "Current ozone depletion is effectively irreversible." All we can do now is sit back and wait to see what happens in the most far-reaching chemistry experiment ever carried out.

CARBON DIOXIDE AND WORLD CLIMATE

The most effective of the atmosphere's greenhouse gases that trap long-wave radiation is carbon dioxide. Other such gases that play a lesser role include CFCs, methane, water vapor, and nitrous oxides. The burning of fossil fuels and the slash-and-burn method of clearing land in some Third World countries have tripled the amount of carbon dioxide in the atmosphere since 1950. The amount of methane, produced by burning fossil fuels, and a trace gas of the air, has doubled since 1850.

The slowly rising global temperature caused by rising concentrations of greenhouse gases is expected to cause the polar ice caps to begin to melt, opening a northwest passage through the Arctic ice and causing a slow rise in sea level that would threaten many of the world's coastal cities. Some experts forecast a rise in sea level of four feet by the year 2050. This warming also would speed the pace of desertification in some regions, with devastating effects on crop yields.

How might a global warming affect animal and plant species? According to a report in the magazine *Science* written by Jean L. Marx, "The warming will be greatest at higher latitudes, which spells trouble for the Arctic tundra and the numerous species, like migratory birds, that depend on it. Coastal organisms will be especially hard hit by rising sea levels and salt water intrusion. In the Northern Hemisphere, forests and other ecosystems will shift northward, and some species at the southern limits of their ranges will die off. Those species now confined to nature reserves—by and large endangered species that nations have labored to protect—will be especially vulnerable as suitable climate and habitat shift out of the reserve borders."

Until the machines of industrial nations began overloading the atmosphere with carbon dioxide, about half remained in the atmosphere while the remaining 50 percent was absorbed by the oceans and forests, especially tropical forests. According to George M. Woodwell, director of the Ecosystems Center at the Marine Biological Laboratory in Woods Hole, Massachusetts, "The emphasis is on the forests because they are extensive in area, conduct more photosynthesis worldwide than any other type of vegetation, and have the potential for storing carbon in quantities that are sufficiently large to affect the carbon dioxide content of the atmosphere." Woodwell also goes on record by saying that "it is difficult to avoid the conclusion that the destruction of the forests of the world is adding carbon dioxide to the atmosphere at a rate comparable to the rate of release for the combustion of fossil fuels," meaning the burning of gasoline by motor vehicles, fuel oil and wood by private homes and industry.

Each year since 1980, according to the United Nations Food and Agricultural Organization, an area the size of Pennsylvania has been deforested in the tropics. Since 1980 about 1.2 billion people have been meeting their fuel-wood needs by cutting down trees faster than the trees can be replaced. In Africa alone about 100 million people are suffering fuel-wood shortages. And the situation becomes worse with Africa's rapidly growing population. On a global level, by the year 2000 there will not be 1.2 billion people cutting down trees to meet their fuel-wood needs but 2.4 billion, according to the FAO.

Before A.D. 900 forests covered 90 percent of Europe. By the year 1900 they covered only 20 percent. According to ecologist Edward J. Kormondy, "in the western llanos or plains of Venezuela 33 percent of the forests were reduced between 1950 and 1975. The total loss of forests worldwide may amount to as much as 1.5 percent a year." However, others disagree, saying that the regrowth of old forests and the increased growth of existing forests may be keeping forest destruc-

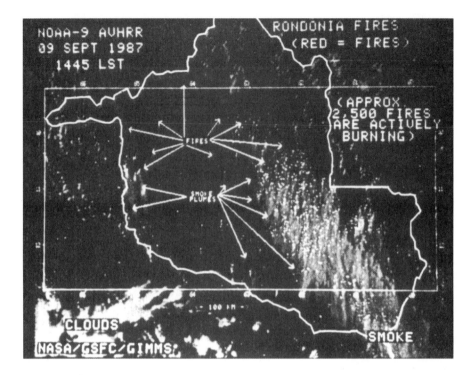

Earth's tropical forests, the richest ecosystems on the planet, are being systematically destroyed at a rate that alarms many ecologists. This satellite image generated from data collected by a weather satellite (NOAA-9) shows some 2,500 forest fires burning in the state of Rondonia, Brazil. The fires are set by small farmers and corporate ranchers to clear space for farming and grazing. Fast food hamburger outlets in the United States are among the major benefactors of this wholesale forest destruction.

tion and regrowth more or less in balance. The cause, they say, is an enriched supply of atmospheric carbon dioxide used by plants for photosynthesis.

Some scientists fear that the drought that gripped the United States in 1988 may have marked a beginning of a warming trend resulting from the buildup of carbon dioxide and other greenhouse gases. If so, by the year 2030 New York may be getting 48 days of summer heat above 90°F instead of 15 days; Chicago 56 instead of 16; Dallas 162 instead of 100; and Los Angeles 27 instead of 5.

Climate is such a complex affair depending on so many factors—

energy cycles of the Sun, global shifts in wind and ocean current patterns, health of the ozone layer, to name a few—that no one can say with certainty what it will be like fifty or a hundred years from now. However, climatologists look for trends, and a buildup of greenhouse gases in the atmosphere unmistakably is occurring and has been for well over a century. Eventually, an increasing accumulation of carbon dioxide in the air must spell heat. The 1980s had the hottest four years of any decade since 1900. On the basis of a warming trend that seems to be speeding up, NASA's climatologist James Hansen has said that he is "99 percent" certain that the greenhouse effect has started. "It has been detected and is changing our climate now," he told a U.S. Senate committee hearing in June 1988. A year later he further told Congress that his computer climate modeling causes him to expect "drought intensification at most middle- and low-latitude land areas." Many of Hansen's colleagues do not share his faith in computer climate models and think that Hansen's long-range weather outlook is questionable. Hansen and his supporters do not agree.

Effects would differ in different parts of the world, according to climatologists. Shifting wind patterns might increase rainfall over parts of Africa that are presently relatively dry, for example. Growing seasons might be lengthened in parts of the Soviet Union, Canada, and Scandinavia. The United States might be less lucky and watch its wheat and corn belts dry up with 40 percent less rainfall than now. Water tables in such regions would lower, and those regions along the coast would find their water supplies useless as they became invaded by salt water. Lake Michigan would begin to evaporate, causing vast areas of reeking mud to surface around Chicago.

What, if anything, can be done to ease the greenhouse effect? In July 1988 some three hundred scientists and government officials from forty-eight countries attended a Toronto, Canada, conference entitled "The Changing Atmosphere." They heard the prime minister of Norway, Gro Harlem Brundtland, plead for corrective action: "For too long . . . we have been playing lethal games with vital life-support systems," she said. "Time has come to start the process of change."

But what kind of changes, and how effective would they be in slowing the greenhouse effect? Today we are adding to the atmosphere's carbon dioxide reservoir at the rate of 4 percent a year. If that *rate* continues, the planet could heat up by 1.5 to 4.5°C by the year 2030. Many experts say that we must try to slow the 4 percent rate. If we could slow it to 2 percent a year the big heat might not come until the year 2050. That twenty-year delay could give us time to breed new crops capable of tolerating heat and drought, to redesign and rebuild selected port cities, and to relocate endangered coastal populations inland.

Unfortunately, the reality of such a cutback in carbon dioxide addition to the air seems remote in view of predictions of a *doubling* of the present rate over the next forty years. The Toronto conference ended on the note that all industrial nations should immediately begin cutting back on fossil fuel emissions, and that wealthy nations should reduce their carbon dioxide emissions 20 percent by the year 2005. Whether that turns out to be manageable, or even possible, remains to be seen.

The collective activity of all large cities creates a dome-shaped microenvironment within which the city's residents work and play. Heat absorbed by asphalt, concrete, and stone of pavements and buildings raises the temperature 1.5° to 2.5°C higher than in the suburbs. Dust, smoke, and other pollutants collect in a city's microenvironment, which tends to remain until broken up by wind or rain. After W. Lowry

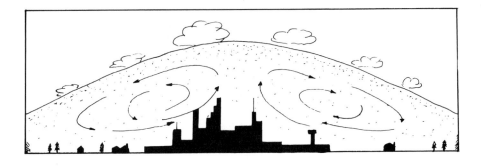

WHEN IT RAINS ACID

Acid rain is any form of precipitation—fog, rain, snow, sleet—that contains high levels of acid. It is caused when precipitation picks up sulfur compounds released from the chimneys of power plants and factories that burn low-quality coal or from active volcanoes, and nitrogen emissions from automobile exhausts, power plants, and other sources. As with carbon dioxide, sulfur and nitrogen emissions have been entering the air in large quantities since about 1850, when the Industrial Revolution was in full force.

Acid rain has killed many lakes and streams of the northeastern United States and has stunted forest growth since at least the 1970s. Although some scientists say that acid rain has let up a bit since around 1980, others do not agree. No matter who is right, the amount of acid raining into our lakes, streams, and forests depends on how rigorously environmental protection regulations are enforced.

Chemists use a scale called the pH scale to measure just how acid a solution is. The lower the number from 1 to 7, the greater the acidity. Glacial ice that formed long before 1850 has a pH above 5, which is about the acidity of milk and human saliva. In February, 1979 the average pH of rain in Toronto was 3.5; in the fall of 1981 fog in Los Angeles had a pH of 2.2. Wheeling, West Virginia holds the record with a pH of 1.4, just above battery acid, which has a pH of 1.0.

Acid rain is produced mainly by industries in the Midwest and is carried eastward by the prevailing westerly winds and deposited in parts of Canada and the Northeast. So destructive is it that in 1975 more than 80 of 214 high-altitude lakes in the Adirondacks had lost all their fish. Half the lakes had a pH of 5 or lower. By the late 1970s nine rivers in Nova Scotia, once abundant with salmon, had a pH lower than 4.7 and no salmon. Acid rain has also severely damaged forests of spruce, pine, aspen, and birch in Germany and elsewhere in Europe.

The case of acid rain is one positive example of how strictly enforced regulations can aid the environment. According to Robert Repetto, "Despite increasing evidence of damage to forests and lakes from acid deposition, rain's acidity and atmospheric concentrations of sulfates and nitrates have not been increasing during the 1980s. The direct cause of these trends is the enforcement of environmental regulations limiting emissions from motor vehicles, industries, electric utilities, municipalities, and other major pollution sources."

All harmful emissions into the environment point up an important moral question: What right does any manufacturer, industry, state, or nation have to pollute the air when that pollution is carried on the wind, crossing state and national boundaries and adversely affecting millions of people helpless to correct the situation? Several paper companies in Maine, for instance, are freely permitted by the state to release from their stacks noxious and corrosive fumes with a strongly offensive odor. Wind often carries the fumes as a huge invisible cloud that drifts on the wind from a Westbrook mill near Portland throughout the city, to the great discomfort of some 100,000 people. Rumford and Jay are two other Maine towns where the paper mill odor is often so bad that it is necessary to drive through town with car windows tightly closed.

One mill worker in Rumford once told me that "the fumes mixed with fog are strong enough to eat the paint off a car." But then he added, "The odor don't bother me none, it smells jobs." The attitude and the disjointed logic of the mill operators in Maine, and in certain other states, is that they are providing jobs and, *therefore,* have an economic right to foul the environment for their profit but to the discomfort of others.

THE QUALITY OF LIFE IN THIRD WORLD COUNTRIES

While environmental quality in some industrialized nations appears to be improving due to the enforcement of environmental regulations, the picture is not rosy in Third World countries, where population growth is the most rapid. According to estimates projected to the year 2025, about 85 percent of population growth in Third World countries will be in the cities, the growth rate being a high 3 percent a year (compared with the 1989 world average of 1.8 percent). Cities with the largest

The stacks of paper mills in Maine and several other states freely pour noxious fumes into the air, and release toxic fluids into rivers, to the discomfort of many thousands of people living within a several-mile radius of the mills. Despite environmental protection regulations, Maine's paper mills continue to pollute the air today as effectively as they did in the 1930s. A combination of economic and political interests makes a cleanup agonizingly slow, and in many cases impossible. Such pollution often is beyond the control of those the pollution most affects.

As human population soars in Third World countries, their cities are hard hit by an increasing inflow of people who can no longer make a living off the land by farming. The result is rapidly growing slums that produce unsanitary conditions and disease brought on by poor water and air quality. In many instances, toxic fluids from factories are dumped along with raw sewage into rivers, canals, and bays. A fresh-water supply in Calcutta, India, shown here, is hard to come by for the teeming millions of poor people. Many die during explosive epidemics of water-borne diseases such as cholera and typhoid.

populations will grow the fastest. In 1985 some 220 million people lived in twenty-eight Third World cities, each with a population of more than 4 million. By the year 2000 we can expect fifty huge Third World cities with a total population of 455 million.

Such rapid growth of Third World cities will have enormous environmental impacts. Almost certainly their already poor water and air quality will be degraded to even lower levels, to levels far below even the minimum health standards set by industrialized nations. In those cities today the poor live in shacks in the back yards of factories or in sprawling slum areas. Waste water from such factories, along with raw sewage from the city, flow untreated into rivers, canals, and bays. Further, most of these countries have few, if any, effective environmental regulations to control any kind of pollution. If conditions do not improve as the populations of Third World cities soar, it is hard to imagine the poverty, misery, and disease that the fouled and crowded environment will cause.

Many leaders of Third World nations think that large populations will be a magical key to becoming a developing nation. They fail to see that the industry needed to raise the standard of living of all those people will, if not controlled by environmental regulations, simply further degrade the environment. Although industrial development since the 1850s has been the immediate cause of environmental degradation, the pressure of expanding populations has, and will continue to be, the force prodding development and eroding the quality of life.

WORLD POPULATION CONTROL

The question is not how many people a city, a nation, or the planet can support, but how many can enjoy a desirable quality of life. In recent years the problem of population growth has become a matter of public policy debate, with much of the discussion focusing on how population growth can be regulated.

"Family planning" is a vague term that means different things to different people. Essentially it means that families are free to plan their size, or to have as many children as they want to have. In most parts of the world families want, and usually have, more children than the replacement value, or the number that would keep the local population at a steady, nongrowing state. That, coupled with the lowering of death rates in Third World countries, clearly means continued population growth.

Part of the idea of family planning is to educate people about how to control the size of their families by not having more children than they want. Such education programs were begun in Third World countries in the early 1960s by international agencies, many national governments, and private foundations. There is no denying that these efforts have generally been instrumental in slowing population growth in some Third World countries as well as in certain developing countries. For example, Edward J. Kormondy reports a survey taken in twenty countries, in nineteen of which (including Mexico, Kenya, Pakistan, Bangladesh, and the Philippines) ". . . three-quarters or more of the women who were or had been married know about contraception. . . . The highest use of contraception was by women in the mid-range of their reproductive years; it was lower among younger and older women. Finally, usage increased with levels of educational attainment, paid employment, and urban residence."

However, there are instances where family planning education programs have not worked as well as hoped for. In Punjab, India, for example, of 5,196 women who sought birth control aid, more than half already had six or more children.

What is the solution for those nations whose populations are so large and growing so rapidly that they cannot feed themselves, or can feed themselves only marginally, or will not be able to feed themselves in another generation? Where voluntary means of controlling population have failed, should such nations impose compulsory control on their population growth? And if they do, is it reasonable to expect couples to be willing to limit family size in accordance with government regulation? What would be the penalties if they did not? Compulsory abortion, compulsory sterilization?

Couples might be rewarded, through tax relief, for *not* having more than one child. In the United States, for example, couples are rewarded for *having* children by receiving on their federal income tax a sizable deduction for each dependent child. China, on the other hand, firmly encourages a "one-child family" by giving those parents strong financial advantages and preference in housing. But despite the slowing growth of China's population, China will have to boost its food production by 50 percent in order to feed the 1,500,000,000 people it is expected to have in the year 2020. That may turn out to be an impossible task.

Many developed nations of the world, including those European countries mentioned earlier, are now demonstrating to undeveloped and developing nations that population can be slowed and controlled by voluntary means. But does it follow that the overpopulated Third World countries can be encouraged to follow that example? Probably not. As you found earlier, there is a tradition for having large families in Third World countries. Further, most Third World governments are convinced that their countries can develop only by increasing their populations. Now add medical and dietary technology from developed nations reducing death rates among the young of poor nations and you can understand how explosive population growth can come about. As an example of medical and dietary technology increasing population growth, Mexico's infant mortality rate of 135 per 1,000 births dropped to 74 in the 1930s and then to 50 in the 1980s. The world average in 1989 was 75.

As William H. McNeill has pointed out, "Doctors and public health officers probably [have] forestalled epidemics that might have checked or even reversed the massive worldwide growth of human population, [thus] distinguishing our age from all that have gone before."

Unfortunately, every year that the world population continues to increase, the risks of widespread and frequent famines, disease, and long-lived ecological disaster also increase. We can only hope that a rational population policy will become a worldwide reality before any such event spells doom on a global scale. But we have no assurance that it will because we do not know if the problem of a runaway world population *can* be solved rationally. A more likely chain of events will be increasing numbers of famines that kill increasing numbers of people in Third World countries, where 10 to 20 million people a year already die of starvation. And as in the past, the response of the rich industrialized nations will be to send temporary food relief that will serve only to keep alive many of those people already living in misery so that they can produce still more offspring. As the economist Kenneth Boulding has pointed out, "If the only check on growth of population is starvation and misery, then any technological improvement [such as a green revolution] will have the ultimate effect of increasing the sum of human misery as it permits a larger proportion to live in precisely the same state of misery and starvation as before the change."

Even the rich industrial nations feel the pinch of too many people, although it has happened so gradually that most of us are not conscious of an erosion of the quality of our lives from one year to the next, or one generation to the next. As Cornell University ecologist Peter Brussard has pointed out, "All of society's present ills—pollution, poverty, racism, social injustice, and war—are further aggravated by an expanding population. All must realize that as the population continues to grow, the standard of living will inevitably go down for all of us. Goods will become increasingly scarce and costs will rise. Pollution will increase, interference and regimentation in our daily lives will increase, and individual privacy and freedom will decrease. Do we want to support many people marginally or fewer people comfortably?"

It's up to us. Or is it?

A P P E N D I X

Dating Once-Living Matter

When archaeologists dig up fossils of living material, they want to know how old the once-living remains are. One means of doing this is the carbon 14 method, an atomic "clock." Because all living matter known to us contains carbon, this chemical element can be used as an atomic clock to date the remains of bone or of charcoal from an ancient camp-fire, for example. Here is how radiocarbon dating works:

Ordinary carbon is in the form of carbon 12. (The number 12 tells us how many of certain particles called protons are contained in the nucleus of each atom.) A heavier form of carbon called carbon 14 is used in radiocarbon dating. Carbon 14 is continually being produced in the atmosphere out of the chemical element nitrogen 14. This happens when nitrogen 14 is bombarded by energetic particles from space, called cosmic rays.

The leaves of all green plants take in carbon 14 from the air, along with carbon 12, as they "breathe in" carbon dioxide day and night. Since almost all animals eat green plants, animals also take in carbon 14.

When a plant or animal dies, it stops taking in carbon. The carbon 14 it has at the time of death then begins to break down. Since carbon 14 decays at a known rate, and the carbon 12 does not decay, carbon 14 can be used as a "clock" that reveals the age of wood, charcoal, peat, bones, marine shells, cloth, and other organic materials.

When an old bone, shell, or other piece of once-living matter being dated is analyzed for age, the scientist compares the number of carbon 14 atoms to the number of carbon 12 atoms. That comparison, or ratio, gives an estimate of the age of the once-living bone or shell. The less carbon 14, the older the bone or piece of shell is. This radiocarbon method of dating once-living matter is reliable for remains up to about 100,000 years old.

GLOSSARY

Amino acids Complex molecules that were among the first molecules of life some four billion or so years ago when Earth had developed a solid crust. Amino acids contain carbon, oxygen, nitrogen, and hydrogen. These molecules are the building blocks of proteins. There are about twenty different kinds of amino acids.

Amphibians That animal group that spends part of its life cycle in water and part on land, including frogs and salamanders, for example. Amphibians lay their eggs in water, where the eggs hatch; the young are fishlike and breathe through gills. Later the young develop into land-dwellers with lungs and four legs.

Anthropology: The study of people, including their social organization, customs and beliefs, language, and physical aspects of people living today and who lived long ago.

Archaeology The study of the history and cultures of peoples who lived in the past by discovering and interpreting the material remains they left behind.

Artifact Any object, either a tool or a weapon, made by human beings. Artifacts include such items as stone tools, projectile points, harpoons, and arrowheads.

Atomic clock   The natural decay, at known rates, of certain radioactive elements such as uranium, potassium, and carbon into other elements. For instance, half the amount of uranium 238 in a sample decays into lead 206 in 4,510 million years; half the amount of carbon 14 in a sample decays into nitrogen 14 in 5,600 years.

Australopithecus   Primitive hominoids ("southern ape-man") who lived in Africa as early as 3.5 million years ago.

Bacteria   Thought to have been the first living cells, composed of DNA, RNA, and protein.

Biogenesis   The principle that life arises only from living things.

Birth rate   The number of births per 1,000 individuals in a population.

Cambrian Period   That geological time period in the Paleozoic Era spanning 80 million years and that lasted from about 580 million to 500 million years ago.

Carrying capacity   The ability of the environment to supply minerals, food, materials for shelter, and other items required by a population for optimum growth and maintenance. When a population's numbers exceeds the carrying capacity of the environment, the population must undergo a decline in the quality of life or move on, if there is a place to move on to.

Cell   The smallest organized unit of living matter recognized by biologists. All living organisms are composed of cells. Some organisms, such as bacteria, are single cells.

Climate   A region's weather averaged over a long span of time. From the Greek word *klima,* meaning "slope" or "incline," and referring to the degree of slant of the Sun's rays relative to Earth's surface.

Cro-Magnon man   Modern man, who replaced Neanderthal man in Europe about 30,000 years ago; in Africa about 60,000 years ago; and in Southeast Asia about 40,000 years ago.

Culture The customs, equipment, techniques, manufactures, ideas, language, and beliefs of a people.

Cuneiform The earliest known true writing, a system of marks made by pressing a wedge into soft clay tablets. Cuneiform writing seems to have been invented by the people of Uruk in the Middle East around 3500 B.C.

Deoxyribonucleic acid (DNA) The substance of genes and the carrier of genetic information in cells, and a supervisor of the manufacturer of protein.

Death rate The number of deaths per 1,000 individuals in a population.

Demography The statistical study of human populations, taking into account their size, growth patterns, distribution, density, and vital statistics.

Desertification The gradual deterioration of fertile land to desert conditions due to natural causes (extended drought), human abuse of the land (overgrazing cattle or unwise farming practices), or a combination of both.

Doubling time The length of time it takes a given population to double its numbers. The doubling time of the world human population in 1986 was forty years, compared with two hundred years in the year 1650.

Ecosystem A community of organisms plus all aspects of the physical environment.

Element A substance made up entirely of the same kinds of atoms. Such a substance cannot be broken down into a simpler substance by chemical means. Examples are gold, oxygen, lead, and chlorine.

Energy That property of an object enabling it to do work. Stars emit huge amounts of energy in the forms of light, heat, radio waves, X rays, and ultraviolet rays, for example.

Evolution The various patterns of biological change that ultimately cause the success (adaptation) or failure (extinction) of species and produce new species of plants and animals. As it has in the past, biological evolution continues to take place today. Charles Darwin and Alfred Russell Wallace are credited with developing the basic principles of evolution.

Extinction The total disappearance of an entire species or higher group of plants or animals. Once a species has become extinct, it is gone forever.

Enuma Elish The world creation myth of the Babylonians, who took the plot from the Sumerians, whom the Babylonians conquered around 2000 B.C. It also goes by the name of the "Babylonian Genesis."

Fertility rate The number of births per 1,000 females age 15 through 49.

Gene That biological unit of inheritance that determines a particular trait, such as hair color, height, and general physical appearance of an individual.

Gene pool The total of all genes (or genotypes) in a given population.

Genetic drift Random changes in gene frequency over time due to chance.

Glacier Any mass of moving land ice formed out of compacted snow. There are eight principal forms of glaciers.

Gondwana A large southern continental land mass, from which the Antarctic continent split some 135 million years ago.

Green revolution The production of high-yield crops through genetic selection and through the use of modern agricultural technology, which includes irrigation, pesticides, fertilizers, and modern farm machinery.

Greenhouse effect The gradual warming of the planet's surface due to carbon dioxide and certain other atmospheric gases increasing in concentration and so acting as a heat trap that prevents long-wave radiation from Earth's surface from escaping off to space. Human activity since the Industrial Revolution around 1800 has created a greenhouse effect which many scientists think may be with us for centuries to come.

Habitat   The environment in which a species lives, together with all the plant and animal organisms to be found there.

Heidelberg man   A descendant of *Homo erectus* discovered in Germany. Like Java man and Peking man, Heidelberg man is about 300,000 years old.

Hypothesis   A scientific hunch, an idea that seems to explain something that can be observed and that can be tested to find out if it does provide an explanation.

Hominoid   Any primate in the human family. Modern humans are the only surviving hominoids. A group known as *Australopithecus* may have been the first true hominoids; they lived as long ago as 5.5 million years, in the late Tertiary Period.

Homo erectus   A group of hominoids that were clearly human, but not yet modern humans. *Homo erectus* hunted, lived in caves, and knew the art of starting fire. The name means "upright man."

Homo habilis   A humanlike species that lived in Africa and Asia some 1.8 million years ago and that gave rise to *Homo erectus*.

Homo sapiens   The group name of modern humans. It means "wise man."

Hunter-gatherers   People who rely on wild game, fruits, and what other wild foods happen to be in season. A hunter-gatherer existence requires less energy than does a way of life that depends on agriculture. Many groups must have been forced into a hunter-gatherer way of life as a result of being displaced from rich environments by stronger groups and thereafter had to content themselves with marginal lands where they had to move often to make ends meet.

Ice age Any extended period of time during which a substantial portion of Earth's surface is covered by "permanent" ice. There have been seven known major ice ages during the past 700,000 years, with the last ice age reaching its peak about 18,000 years ago.

Java man A descendant of *Homo erectus* first discovered by Eugene Dubois in 1891.

Mammal Any vertebrate animal that has warm blood and a covering of hair, that gives birth to its young (with two exceptions), and that suckles its young.

Melanin A pigment that causes dark skin and that provides some protection from ultraviolet radiation from the Sun.

Molecule Two or more atoms bonded chemically, such as sodium chloride (NaCl) or molecular oxygen (O_2).

Mutation A random, or chance, change in a plant or animal's genes that makes the organism different in one or more ways from its parents. Most mutations are harmful, although many throughout the course of evolution have proven to be beneficial. Mutations may be passed on to offspring.

Myth Any story or other form of explanation for an event, or supposed event, that draws on supernatural causes as opposed to natural causes. The Greek, Roman, American Indian, and many myths of numerous other cultures have enriched world literature and served as a vehicle of the creative expression of human thought.

Neanderthal man Large-jawed people who lived across Europe into the Near East and into central Asia. About five feet tall, they were strong and had large bones. They became extinct about 35,000 years ago.

Ozone layer A layer of heavy oxygen located in the upper atmosphere. The ozone layer consists of triatomic oxygen (O_3) as opposed to diatomic oxygen. This heavy oxygen shields living organisms at Earth's surface from an overexposure to harmful ultraviolet radiation from the Sun.

Paleo-Indians   Any of those groups of people who entered the Americas from Asia up to 5,000 B.C. and who hunted now extinct or locally exterminated animals. Most researchers think that the Paleo-Indians crossed over to the New World over a sprawling land bridge that existed near the end of the last glacial period. Recent evidence suggests that Paleo-Indians may have been in South America at least 60,000 years ago.

Parallel evolution   When two different species evolve similar structures with similar functions due to common selection pressures of their environment. The streamlined shape and swimming appendages of sharks and porpoises are an example; another is the keen vision and adept use of tentacles by squids and octopuses.

Peking man   A descendant of *Homo erectus* first discovered in China in the 1920s by Davidson Black. Peking Man is about 300,000 years old.

Precambrian Era   That geologic time span from 4.6 billion years ago—the estimated age of Earth—to 580 million years ago. The Precambrian is generally viewed as the time when life was firmly establishing itself on Earth.

Protein   A class of large-molecule organic compounds made up of amino acids.

Race   A "race" within any species can be thought of as a group of populations that have certain physical and genetic characteristics in common and that set that group of populations apart from all other populations of the same species. Most anthropologists recognize three races of human beings—Caucasoid (light-skinned), Negroid (dark-skinned), and Mongoloid (intermediate with high cheekbones). There are five races if the Australian aborigines and American Indians are counted as separate races.

Radioactive dating   Determining the age of a substance by the study of the ratio of stable "daughter" elements to their radioactive "parent" element.

Ramapithecus   An advanced ape—not a primitive human—that lived in Africa, Asia, Greece, Turkey, and Hungary some 6 to 8 million years ago.

Reptile   A cold-blooded vertebrate, such as lizards, snakes, and alligators, for example. The Cretaceous Period marked the peak of the reptiles' success with the dominance of the dinosaurs, which were reptiles.

Ribonucleic acid (RNA)   A nucleic acid that is important in the manufacture of protein in cells.

Spontaneous generation   The erroneous belief that living things are created out of decaying meat, mud, dust or the like. The idea had supporters from at least the time of Aristotle until the French scientist Louis Pasteur put the notion to rest once and for all around 1850.

Total fertility rate   The average number of children a woman may be expected to have during her childbearing years.

Ultraviolet radiation (UV)   Harmful radiation of short wavelength from the Sun that in excessive amounts damages the tissues of animals and plants. UV is what gives you sunburn.

Zero population growth   Stabilizing population by bringing into the world only enough individuals to replace those who die, and maintaining that 1:1 ratio. As of 1989, six nations had achieved zero population growth.

F U R T H E R ◇ R E A D I N G

BOOKS

Brown, Lester R., et al. *State of the World: A Worldwatch Institute Report on Progress Toward a Sustainable Society*. New York: W. W. Norton, 1986.

Bryson, Reid A., and Thomas J. Murray. *Climates of Hunger*. Madison, Wisconsin: The University of Wisconsin Press, 1977.

Eckholm, Erik, and Lester R. Brown. *Worldwatch Paper 13: Spreading Deserts—The Hand of Man*, Washington, D.C.: Worldwatch Institute, 1977.

Ehrlich, Paul R., and Anne H. Ehrlich. *Population, Resources, Environment: Issues in Human Ecology*. San Francisco: W. H. Freeman, 1970.

Feshback, Murray. *The Soviet Union: Population Trends and Dilemmas*. Washington, D.C.: Population Reference Bureau, Inc., Vol. 37, No. 3, August, 1982.

Gallant, Roy A. *Ancient Indians*. Hillside, N.J.: Enslow Publishers, 1988.

———. *Earth's Changing Climate*. New York: Four Winds Press, 1979.

———. *Lost Cities*. New York: Franklin Watts, 1985.

Hawkes, Jacquetta. *The First Great Civilizations*. New York: Alfred A. Knopf, 1973.

Hawking, Gerald S. *Stonehenge Decoded*. Garden City, New York: Doubleday, 1965.

Kormondy, Edward J. *Concepts of Ecology*, 4th ed. Englewood Cliffs, N.J.: Prentice-Hall, Inc., 1990.

Lovelock, James. *The Age of Gaia*. New York: W. W. Norton, 1988.

McNeil, William H. *Plagues and Peoples*. Garden City, N.Y.: Anchor Press/Doubleday, 1976.

Murphy, Francis X. *Catholic Perspective on Population Issues II*. Washington, D.C.: Population Reference Bureau, Inc., Vol. 35, No. 6, February, 1981.

1989 World Population Data Sheet. Washington, D.C.: Population Reference Bureau, Inc., 1989.

Pfeiffer, John E. *The Emergence of Humankind*, 4th ed. New York: Harper & Row, 1985.

——— . *The Emergence of Society*. New York: McGraw-Hill, 1977.

——— . *The Creative Explosion*. New York: Harper & Row, 1982.

Repetto, Robert. *Population, Resources, Environment: An Uncertain Future*. Washington, D.C.: Population Reference Bureau, Inc., Vol. 42, No. 2, July 1987.

Ryan, Lyndall. *The Aboriginal Tasmanians*. Vancouver: University of British Columbia Press, 1983.

Schneider, Stephen H. *Global Warming: Are We Entering the Greenhouse Century?* New York: Random House/Sierra Club Books, 1989.

Soldo, Beth J., and Emily M. Agree. *America's Elderly*. Washington, D.C.: Population Reference Bureau, Inc., Vol. 43, No. 3, September 1988.

Sweden Faces Zero Population Growth. Washington, D.C.: Population Reference Bureau, Inc., Vol. 35, No. 2, June 1980.

Tien, H. Yuan. *China: Demographic Billionaire*. Washington, D.C.: Population Reference Bureau, Inc., Vol. 38, No. 2, April 1983.

Toynbee, Arnold. *Cities of Destiny*. New York: McGraw-Hill, 1967.

U.S. Population: Where We Are; Where We're Going. Washington, D.C.: Population Reference Bureau, Inc., Vol. 37, No. 2, June 1982.

van de Kaa, Dirk. *Europe's Second Demographic Transition*. Washington, D.C.: Population Reference Bureau, Inc., Vol. 41, No. 1, March 1987.

ARTICLES

Anderson, Harry, et al. "The Global Poison Trade." *Newsweek,* 7 November 1988, pp. 66–68.

Begley, Sharon, et al. "A Long Summer of Smog." *Newsweek,* 29 August 1988, pp. 46–48.

Bloom, Barry R. "A New Threat to World Health." *Science,* 1 January 1988, p. 9.

Booth, William. "Monitoring the Fate of the Forests from Space." *Science,* 17 March 1989, pp. 1428–29.

Bower, B. "Stone Blades Yield Early Cultivation Clues." Science, 18 February 1989, p. 101.

Cowley, Geoffrey, et al. "Ozone Breakaway." *Newsweek,* 29 August 1988, pp. 48–49.

Easterbrook, Gregg. "Cleaning Up." *Newsweek,* 24 July 1989, pp. 26–42.

Kerr, Richard A. "How to Fix the Clouds in Greenhouse Models. *Science,* 6 January 1989, pp. 28–29.

———. "The Global Warming Is Real." *Science,* 3 February 1989, p. 603.

———. "Hansen vs. the World on the Greenhouse Threat." *Science,* 2 June 1989, pp. 1040–43.

Lewin, Roger. "Life History Patterns Emerge in Primate Study." *Science,* 23 December 1988, pp. 1636–37.

Monastersky, Richard. "Decline of the CFC Empire." *Science News,* 9 April 1988, pp. 234–36.

———. "Global Change: The Scientific Challenge." *Science News,* 15 April 1989, pp. 232–35.

Peterson, Ivars. *Science News,* 24 & 31 December 1988, pp. 408–409.

Putnam, John J. "The Search for Modern Humans." *National Geographic,* October 1988, pp. 439–477.

Raloff, Janet. "Where Acids Reign." *Science News,* 22 July 1989, pp. 56–58.

Roberts, Leslie. "Hard Choices Ahead on Biodiversity." *Science,* 30 September 1988, pp. 1759–61.

———. "Is There Life After Climate Change?" *Science,* 18 November 1988, pp. 1010–12.

Scientific American, a special-topic issue, "Managing Planet Earth." September 1989.

"Toxins, Toxins Everywhere." *Newsweek,* 1 August 1988, pp. 43–48.

Trenberth, Kevin E., et al. "Origins of the 1988 North American Drought." *Science,* 23 December 1988, pp. 1640–45.

White, Peter T. "Rain Forests." *National Geographic,* January 1983, pp. 2–48.

World Watch, January/February 1989. This issue of the bimonthly magazine, published by Worldwatch Institute, Washington, D.C., includes articles on acid rain, dangers from plutonium, deforestation, food, population growth, and global warming.

INDEX